AGENCIES & BRANDS IN THE EXPERIENCE ECONOMY:

MANAGEMENT ORGANIZATION

REPORT & BLUEPRINT

–

MIRCO PASQUALINI

-

Reframe Brands, Marketing & Communication

ISBN: 9781792888861

Released January 2019

Introduction

—

You can love or disagree with different perspectives, but they always trigger a change of thinking.

About this blueprint

Everyone working in the space of brands, marketing and communications has seen their job change rapidly in recent years. In particular, the agency business has been forced to rethink and redefine its role.

As well, the impact of the new economy and the establishment of the experience economy model has changed everything we have known about marketing, brands, customer perspectives and the rules & dynamics defining the relationship between these elements.

All big ad holdings, such as **WPP, Omnicom Group, Publicis Groupe, IPG** and **Detsu**, are running deep transformations, including all their agencies. On the other side, new players and consultancies are growing and gaining business from the agencies, from different perspectives.

The exponential technology innovation and the reshaping of marketing and communication dynamics created new opportunities and business, while at the same time destabilizing agency assumptions.

The big four **(Google, Amazon, Facebook, Apple)** have become the new ads media system, and have been accused for a long time to be a cause of the decline of the big ad holdings. **Consultancies** are growing and expanding their capabilities and as a result, they are earning a part of the big client business typical of large agencies, while **small emerging studios** are rising and innovating from the bottom.

The struggle of the big agencies has been taking place for years and their successful heritage has been the biggest friction to change and adapting to the new scenario.

Multidisciplinary & inclusion have become mandatory requirements for everyone, dethroning traditional "Creatives" from the leadership to a more equal level with other disciplines & practices.

Data & Technology have become the new language; **Design & Experience** are the new religions; a **new generation of leadership** is rising with a system consciousness as an effect of the digital age.

As a result of these shifts, talent spends a lot of time defending their beliefs inside organizations, instead of spending all their energy to be effective with their projects and clients.

Agency leadership is often accused by observers of an absence of a holistic vision, but according to some experts these errors come when "companies continue to make the choices that have guaranteed success in the past, ignoring that the world has changed."

In 1990, the economist **Rebecca Henderson** explained that "the leading companies in the market tend to decline when a business requires their deep reorganization." A deep reorganization / transformation never works when imposed from the top (or at least doesn't reach the results desired), but can truly change everything when grown organically across the entire structure.

How is that done? Those who are working for and with brands need a new way of thinking, not only how to go to market, but also, how to change their way of working every day internally.

How can company management organization be **more holistic, multidisciplinary, integrated, human-centered, systematic, inclusive** and create the conditions to trigger innovation?

In some cases, there is no one solution to fit all organizational challenges. However, this blueprint offers an alternative way of thinking on how to organize teams in this complex scenario and achieve results in a different way.

-

I truly believe in the power of sharing to make changes, and this is the reason why I am sharing this work.

After spending the last 20 years in different business contexts as a consultant for private companies and startups; as a chief design officer for a venture incubator and an executive for agencies, I decided to summarize everything I have observed and discovered about the relationships between companies, teams, operational models, business results and growth in this blueprint.

I do not expect everyone to agree with my work and my vision won't be a fit for all, but I am sure that everyone will find something in these pages useful and different from their perspective capable of stimulating questions or reflections.

A dance teacher told me once, "All movement starts from the feet. Whatever style and technique you want to learn, start to learn how the feet move. They make things happen."

To create a great and innovative business, you must be focused not on designing it, but designing to create the conditions that happen, and transforming how an organization works (the feet) is a mandatory step to innovate a business (the body).

REPORT

Experience economy & brands

—

In the experience economy, it doesn't matter how good your product or service is — the experience you provide for your customers ultimately defines the heart and soul of your brand.

What is the experience economy? Why does it matter?

More than 20 years have passed since **Joseph Pine II** and **Jim Gilmore** introduced the concept of "**Experience Economy**" that identified and described a phenomenon that was only at the beginning stages and that grew more and more.

Here's how they introduced it with simple words that anyone can understand:

> "How do economies change? The entire history of economic progress can be recapitulated in the four-stage evolution of the birthday cake. As a vestige of the agrarian economy, mothers made birthday cakes from scratch, mixing farm commodities (flour, sugar, butter, and eggs) that together cost mere dimes.
>
> As the goods-based industrial economy advanced, moms paid a dollar or two to Betty Crocker for premixed ingredients. Later, when the service economy took hold, busy parents ordered cakes from the bakery or grocery store, which, at $10 or $15, cost ten times as much as the packaged ingredients.
>
> Now, in the time-starved 1990s, parents neither make the birthday cake nor even throw the party. Instead, they spend $100 or more to "outsource" the entire event to Chuck E. Cheese's, the Discovery Zone, the Mining Company, or some other business that stages a memorable event for the kids—and often throws in the cake for free."

Staging experiences to sell in a sophisticated economy is not unusual and is not an amorphous construct; it is as real an offering as any service, good, or commodity. In today's service economy, many companies simply wrap experiences around their traditional offerings to sell them better. To realize the full benefit of staging experiences, however, businesses must deliberately design engaging experiences that command a fee.

This transition from selling services/products to selling experiences will be no easier for established companies to undertake and weather than the last great economic shift, from the industrial to the service economy.

Brands also have a hard time understanding how to deal with the new scenario, where everything matters, where **customers play, as an actor, multiple roles on the same stage**, experiencing the brand through multiple touch points.

In this scenario, audiences are showing new economic behaviors, a new way of making choices and redefining priorities, a new way of thinking that changes everything we have known about brands, marketing & communication.

More Insights
(Search the following sentence in Google to retrieve the link)

* **Amazon - The Experience Economy, by Joseph Pine & Jim Gilmore**

* **HBR - Design a customer experience transformation**

From one system to the system of the systems

The new economy and the proliferation of digital business through mobile apps, web platforms and IoT objects have brought to the masses the perception of having a system around – a system of interconnected digital data and objects that cooperate with each other and work for us.

'The rise of the system consciousness is what identifies not only the new generations, but also the other generations living in this century.

Today, the **World Wide Web** has become the "**Whatever, Whenever, Wherever you want**" system, which integrates and distributes everything, where the **media system** remains, but as part of a larger system, which includes millions of other micro systems.

The consumer is thus in a position to observe what is happening around him/her with a more holistic, more central and decisional perspective than marginal and as a spectator.

Today, brands take shape and communicate not only through the media system, but also through the system that the audience creates and chooses around it.

In traditional marketing this becomes an apparent fragmentation of the control and management of the brand. In modern marketing this is called "audience/customer experience," a multidisciplinary, holistic, inclusive, human-centered but above all, a system-focused approach.

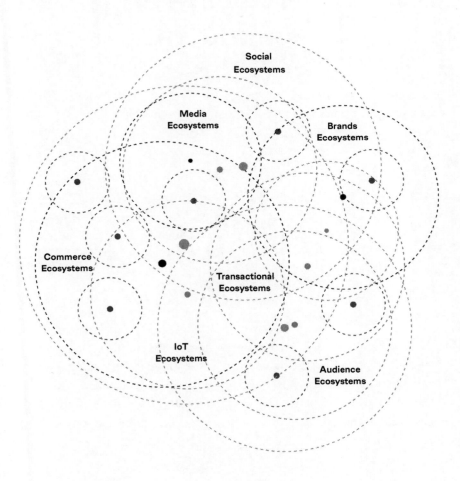

The consequences of the experience economy for brands & marketing

The factors that indicate the increasing propagation of an experience economy are numerous and increasingly frequent in every business category. In order to offer an experience, both as a business and as a brand, the attention of every initiative is oriented towards establishing a solid long-term relationship with its audience.

And thanks to this form of relationship, through technologies such as Machine Learning and Augmented Intelligence, we can become proactive by anticipating not only the needs of the consumer, but also his/her fears or desires, transforming the marketing from "curative" to "preventive," from "intrusive" to "useful."

But there are many other consequences of this new way of doing business. **Here are some of them:**

- **New business models are rising:** Businesses that require a long-term relationship require new monetization and optimization models. Here are the forms, such as the **Subscription models** (eg: Amazon Prime, Apple program, Netflix) or the **Sharing models** (eg: UBER, AirBnb), that have become more and more frequent in an experience stage.

- **Hype by advertising vs. audience sharing:** In an experiential model, traditional advertising becomes inefficient, as it is not easily contextualized and **authentic in conversation**, unlike the buzz generated and shared by the audience itself. Let us remember that conversation and narratives are the elements that determine the rhythm and participation of the audience in a context of experience. Here is an example of how Tesla, with an "Ad for Vehicle" budget of zero, has remained the brand with the greatest equity in online research for a long time.

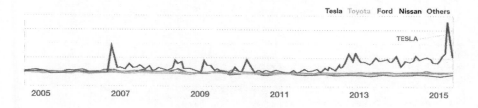

GOOGLE TRENDS: INTEREST OVER TIME
Indexed Search Volume Compared to Changes
in Interest in Auto & Vehicle category 2005–2017
Source: Gartner L2

Tesla Toyota Ford Nissan Others

TESLA

2005   2007   2009   2011   2013   2015

AD SPENDING PER VEHICLE SOLD
2014 – Measured Media Spend in USD Millions Divided by Vehicles Sold
Data Source: Gartner L2

Toyota	Honda	Ford	Tesla
$367	$313	$258	

- **Democratization of innovation:** In a context of Business and Brands, what innovates is no longer just technology, a patent, or a product, rather **it's how things are done** and as a result an experience takes shape in the system around our audience. This is why innovating today becomes more accessible and democratic, where anyone as a single person or small business has the opportunity to innovate equally with a large company (eg. Dollar Shave Club, Warby Parker).

DOLLAR SHAVE CLUB   WARBY PARKER

- **Brand vs Experience equity:** Audiences are less attached to brands and more attached to experiences. Are you buying products on Amazon because you love Amazon as a brand or because it make your life easier? This is a growing trend as recent surveys have shown:

PERCENTAGE OF AFFLUENTS WHO CAN IDENTIFY A "FAVORITE" BRAND
USA, Top 5% by Household Income (HHI) (2007-2015)
Data Source: Gartner L2

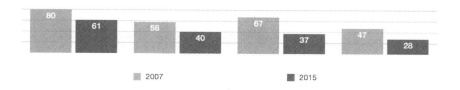

2007   2015

- **New meaning for what makes a brand:** People want–and expect–more from the brands they buy. They want to support mission-based companies such as **Patagonia,** companies as on demand as **Postmates,** and companies with products as dependable as **Apple.** What makes a brand today spans from visual identity to the business model, from ethics to interfaces, from the way they work to the narrative used through all the touch points with their customers. In other words, the experience of living with that brand.

- **From the information to reputation age:** The beginning of the millennium was called the "age of information" because with the spread of access to the network and the sharing of content, everything became available to anyone. Today the great challenge is to navigate, evaluate and select in this flood of information we are subjected to every day; and that is how the synthesis (or reputation) of what spreads in the network, as a form of conversation, becomes more revealing than anything else. In an experience economy context, the **authenticity** of information becomes **more important** than information itself.

- **Discovery vs Advertising:** More and more, results show us how living within a complex experiential system becomes difficult for leading and engaging audiences with traditional forms of communication, often reduced to act as "noise." Sensible growth is from Brands that are not spending in Advertising, but that are moving more money in the forms of "consumer discovery" (eg. Instagram, reviews, content as stories, pop-up experiences, etc.) joining the conversations rather than interrupting them.

COSMETIC INDUSTRY Q1 2015 vs Q1 2017
Data Source: Gartner L2

ELC Top 15 Makeup Brands	
MAC	-1.5
Clinique	-1.1
Estée Lauder	-0.6
Bobbi Brown	-0.3
Smashbox	+0.1
-3.4%	

Other Makeup Top 15	
Urban Decay	+0.7
Lancôme	-0.6
Benefit	-0.2
Bare Essentials	-1.3
Chanel	-0.4
NARS	
-2.5%	

Top 15 Makeup Indies	
Anastasia	+1.5
Tarte	+1.0
Too Faced	+1.0
+3.5%	

- **Ad business is downsizing:** Everyone knows this, and it reflects as well in the budgets for the Agency, but more shocking are the forecasts for the Ad trend investment, which are supposed to become half in the next six years*. Is Ad business going to die? Of course not; it will be different, integrated, less advertising but more a trans-medial storytelling practice. What will we call it? Right now, it is hard to bet.

Forecast provided by Gartner L2

TOP-10 US BEAUTY INDUSTRY ADVERTISERS, BY TRADITIONAL MEDIA AD SPEND
Percent Change 2014 vs 2015
Data Source: Gartner L2

	2014	2015	% Change
L'Oreal	1,346	1,198	-11.0%
P&G	799.6	572.2	-28.4%
J&J	389.6	389.0	-.2%
Unilever	398.3	266.6	-10.6%
Estée Lauder	222.8	244.4	+9.7%
Genomma Lab	88.5	167.7	+89.5%
Coty	199.9	165.5	-17.2%
Revlon	164.9	153.2	-7.1%
LVMH	109.8	114.5	+4.3%
Kao	102.1	103.2	+1.1%
TOTAL	$4.689,9	$4.508,0	-4.1%

- **Susceptible audience:** Comparing experiences has become more and more frequent. Just think of mobility solutions: in a city like New York besides **UBER**, there are other experiences like **Lyft**, **Via**, **Curb**, **Juno**, **Arro**, **Maven**, **Car2Go**, etc.–a series of brands operating in the same business where the audience moves from platform to platform as soon as the experience received does not match expectations, regardless of the relationship with the brand itself.

- **New benchmarks are in the experience landscape, not in your business category anymore:** Whenever a better experience is released in the market, it automatically becomes the experiential model reference, not only in the same business context but also in others. Audiences understand the value of the experience not the complexity of technology behind or the business perspective that generates it. In this way, your next benchmark probably will be in another business category.

- **Retailers that are not part of a holistic digital-physical experience are dying:** Listing the specific reasons why we have witnessed the decline of many retail brands like Sears in recent years is not easy because each case is very different, but they have one thing in common: the lack of a coordinated holistic experience. On the contrary, other brands such as **Apple**, **Walmart** and **Nike** managed to create an integrated experience that allowed them to transit into the experience economy, while brands like **Amazon** are trying to balance themselves through more and more acquisitions and retail initiatives to grow their authenticity.

More Insights
(Search the following sentence in Google to retrieve the link)

- 'A world with no ads': P&G, Unilever's top marketers envision different paths forward

Data, experience and audience conversation

Everyday in the world **2.5 trillion data** are produced in the commercial context, and brands still have trouble understanding completely their audience.

Data is the most powerful element we can use to understand, discover and react in real time to every change happening in a multidimensional experience system around customers, but at the same time we are aware that without data or when referenced in the wrong context, data become useless.

From a brand perspective, to grow the engagement and the participation of its audience, understanding people's economic and life behaviors is not enough to add value to their experience, because factors such as fear, desire, anxiety, loss, excitement, etc. cannot be tracked in these contexts.

We can hypothesize and we can bet, but these factors, essential to making every marketing action useful and creating trust and strong relationships with the brand in an experience stage, need a specific context: the "conversation."

Conversation is the narrative of any form of experience and the only context we should use to give a meaning to any data. In the conversation, we have all the information needed to collect insights about the **feelings of our audience, where they are thinking to go, what they are thinking they should do and how.**

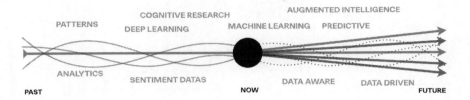

DATA AND TECHNOLOGIES
(Positions of specific words in the timeline are only for explicative purposes)

Future forms of machine learning, cognitive technologies and A.I. will definitely lead what marketing should and will do, more effectively, more reactionary, more efficiently by connecting human behaviors in multiple spaces, such as empathetical, economical, etc. But to be clear, this doesn't mean marketing agencies will not have a future.

Agencies will play a huge role in helping brands develop their own brand conversation system to be resilient, consistent and authentic; able to lead experiences, increase engagement, audience participation and give a new dimension and a real value to business data.

The decline of the customer experience (CX) value

Customer experience performance is flat for the third year in a row after rising for years. CX results show a dangerous gap in customers' sense of emotional engagement and loyalty. **And 89% of surveyed CX professionals state that the ROI of CX is not well established** in their companies. Across Forrester's Customer Experience Index (CX IndexTM), few businesses made real gains, most continue to plateau, and some fell back.

The results are at the same time shocking and unsurprising: companies are struggling to create human connections that matter. We are living in a market where customers are increasingly free agents and where adoption and abandonment occur at a fast pace and with little regret. If we don't understand why this is happening, it means we are missing something, we are missing a perspective.

Customer initiatives and loyalty programs are designed to confront free agent dynamics, whether that means minimizing churn or inspiring the next investment or spend. The ideal, of course, is to create sustained loyal relationships.

However, our CX Index results suggest that these programs are not working as planned. While customers are broadly satisfied with the core services and products of the respective industries, they generally don't perceive that their existing levels of loyalty are rewarded. In other words, if loyalty is an economic engine, that engine is sputtering.

Switching from a Customer-centric perspective (brand-client business context) to a more **holistic Human-centric** perspective (more inclusive context), it seems to always become the growing trend to build trust and a strong loyalty with the audience.

Forrester 2017 and 2018 CX Index Results

Source: Forrester Analytics Customer Experience Index Online Survey, US Consumers 2017 and 2018

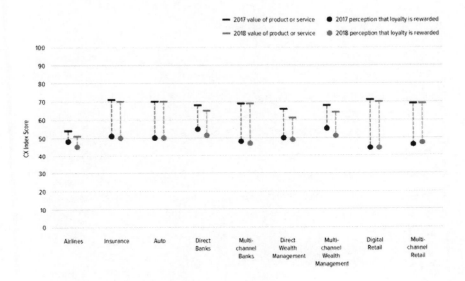

More Insights
(Search the following sentence in Google to retrieve the link)

- **Forbes - There are bo clear CX leaders among US brands – for the third year in a row**

- **Forrester - Customer experience index reveals brands lack human connectionar CX leaders among US brands**

The rise of the employee experience (EX) value

Now that, according to Gartner, more than 90% of businesses compete primarily on the basis of customer experience (CX), it's no longer enough to make CX a corporate priority. The next competitive frontier is employee experience (EX) and the signs indicate so strongly that EX will become the next priority for organizations that I'm calling 2019 "The Year of Employee Experience."

EX is the sum of everything an employee experiences throughout his or her connection to the organization—every employee interaction, from the first contact as a potential recruit to the last interaction after the end of employment.

Why is Employee Experience important?

EX is essential to increase not only employee satisfaction, productivity, and retention, but also sustainable growth, competitive advantage, and brand equity.

And it does not only concern aspects related to recruitments or public reviews on **Glassdoor** and **LinkedIn**, but to those of business performance, growth, and competitive advantage. Just think of the **UBER** case as the brake produced as a result of an unsatisfactory EX between 2017 and 2018, which led first to a change of CEO and then to a complete strategic change in its brand and positioning to return to growth.

In research conducted by **Jacob Morgan** he finds:

> "...experiential organizations had more than **4 times the average profit** and more than **2 times the average revenue**. They were also almost **25 percent smaller**, which suggests higher levels of productivity and innovation."

Many agencies are already pushing into this space, integrating skills not common to the traditional world of communications, such as behavioral science and change management, under the hat of the Employee Experience.

Where traditional consulting companies focus on efficiency and performance, agencies can fill that gap, that lack of assessment of the impact that a good or negative employee experience can have in terms of brand equity, customer experience and growth.

We live in an economy model where we sell experiences and we build stages for experiences through a working experience.

More Insights
(Search the following sentence in Google to retrieve the link)

- **HBR - Why the millions we spend on employee engagement buy us so little?**

- **Forrester - Digital transformation: why culture is so key**

- **Forrester - Employee experience powers the future of work**

- **ReCode - Drivers don't trust Uber.**

B2B marketing is in limbo

"Crap" Content continues to describe B2B marketing. For the third consecutive year, B2B marketing content continues to underwhelm business consumers — most say vendors give them too much material and much of that material is useless.

B2B firms are engaged in a content arms race, trying to achieve competitive advantage by producing any possible content that any possible buyer could possibly need at any possible time. However, as velocity points out, battling for numerical content superiority means nothing if your content isn't relevant or interesting to buyers.

B2B marketing has been under pressure for several years. Far too many marketing shops are optimized to supply-side market operations and behavior, and are struggling with foundational issues such as data; grappling with an inefficient and ad hoc technology architecture; and failing to pivot to customer-led marketing.

B2B marketers are trying to drive growth with existing tools, people, data realities, and processes while preparing for a world where buyers behave more like consumers and where operations premised on scale will move to operations driven by human empathy and individualization (**buyer's experience**).

.

[1] Considering the materials you receive from vendors, how much do you agree with the following statements about the content you are provided?
(On a scale of 1 [completely disagree] to 5 [completely agree]

Source: Forrester Consulting's Q1 2018 Global Marketing Content Credibility Study

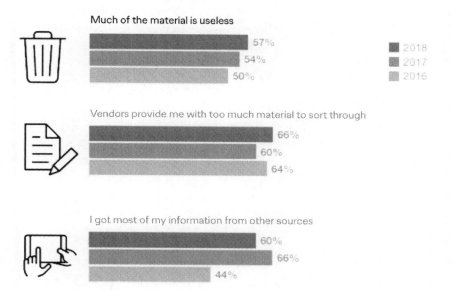

Much of the material is useless

57%
54%
50%

■ 2018
■ 2017
■ 2016

Vendors provide me with too much material to sort through

66%
60%
64%

I got most of my information from other sources

60%
66%
44%

More Insights
(Search the following sentence in Google to retrieve the link)

- **Forrester - Credible, empathetic content wins over elusive B2B buyers**

How marketing perspectives have changed

In this complex context of the experience economy, even the perspective with which marketing has always worked has changed to adapt to a systematic environment with its new rules.

A total paradigm shift:

- **From observational to *data driven*:** Thanks to more and more sophisticated technologies able to produce and analyze faster more data, such as Machine Learning and forms of Augmented Intelligence, every marketing action is no longer born from behavioral observations of people and the market. Today every creative idea or opportunity must be validated or identified through data, a method often criticized for lack of humanity and serendipities. More often agencies will be able to value the data in the context of the brand conversation with their audience, developing new skills and methodologies.

- **From curative to *preventive*:** Marketing is now developing a new way of thinking, no longer solving problems on retrospective insights such as sales patterns over the same period, or on case-histories of other businesses and brands, but on future forecasts. The new role of marketing is not to treat existing problems, but to prevent the development of trends that could lead to future problems. Marketing thus assumes a role as a coach, which in turn requires an integrated relationship with its customers.

- **From fragmented to *integrated*:** As already mentioned, to give value to the brand in an experience economy context, we must focus on distributing value within that system that represents the perspective of its audience. Marketing must acquire methods and processes that allow the articulation of integrated, multidisciplinary solutions able to escape from the risk of being trapped between silos of vertical skills and orchestrating everything by validating their intentions in a systematic way.

- **From a feature value to *an experience value*:** We are already seeing this in some business categories, some with incredibly fast changes. From Healthcare to Wellness, from Automotive to Mobility, the value of what one sells, promotes or promises is no longer the benefit that a product, technology or offer has, but the power to change or transform what we offer through the audience experience.

- **From short-term to *long-term relationships*:** New tactics are necessary in the marketing world to interact successfully with the audience as the results will be less and less measured in "leads" but increasingly in "audience participation" in the whole brand system experience. Keeping your audience active and enjoying the benefits of the system will enable you to influence and invite other participants to join, establishing a new strength of relationship between brand and audience: less and less consumers, more and more participants of an experience.

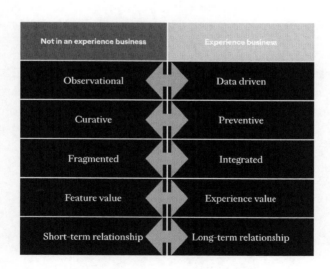

How have consumer perspectives changed?

Customers have also changed, their perspectives have changed and the way they make their choices, compare solutions and evaluate brands. This is because with the new dynamics of a system experience, it changes the point of view from which choices are made–more central, more holistic, more in control of what happens:

- **From better tools to *a better way of doing*:** it does not matter if a product has a better engine or a more advanced camera. Today what sells is the factor of not having to deal with car maintenance or to be able to shoot better even at night.

- **From what will be delivered to *the value of the impact of what will be delivered:*** it is no longer relevant what the product is in itself, but the value that the impact of having it has in our lives or in the context of experience. (ex: from a phone with a 24 megapixels camera, to a phone with a camera for better selfies.)

- **From tailored to *my needs to useful to me*:** Audiences are aware of the power of data and how everything is interconnected. For this reason, we have stopped thinking about what we need, and more and more the focus is on whether something is useful, effectively translating the digital models of personalization into business, communication and real life; resulting in a change of expectations.

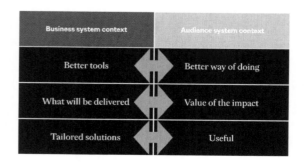

Target audience: from generations to behavioral adopters

Generations are never targets. Another mistake of our times is the assumption of identifying specific generations as targets of marketing operations. Just think to what extent **Millennials** or **Generation X** are still being discussed.

But in an economic model organized around system dynamics, a system fueled by human choices and behaviors is perpetually mutating and in a context of economic behaviors, the behavior of the audience grows, spreads and dies exactly like a virus.

Here the generations, instead of being seen as a target to be reached, should be considered similarly to the early or laters adopters of new behavior that, if improved and effective, are spread also through other generations (ex: Millennials as Explorers).

These are common concepts in the world of technology and data, but not yet integrated in the world of communications and marketing. Agencies can play an advantageous role in developing new forms of business narratives, methodologies and tactics to act in this perspective giving value to the brands.

Explorers	Early Adopters	Early Majority	Late Majority	Later Followers
% Adoption value impact				% Adoption frictions
Niches		Main Market		
Maintain a social status	More efficiency	Exponential opportunities	Transformative needs	Necessary

Type of adopters:

- **Explorers**: are willing to take risks, have the highest social status, have financial liquidity, are social and have closest contact to scientific sources and interaction with other innovators. Theirs risk tolerance allows them to adopt technologies that may ultimately fail. Financial resources help absorb these failures.

- **Early Adopters:** These individuals have the highest degree of opinion leadership among the adopter categories. Early adopters have a higher social status, financial liquidity, advanced education and are more socially forward than late adopters. They are more discreet in adoption choices than innovators. They use judicious choice of adoption to help them maintain a central communication position.

- **Early Majority:** They adopt an innovation after a varying degree of time that is significantly longer than the innovators and early adopters. Early Majority have above average social status, contact with early adopters and seldom hold positions of opinion leadership in a system.

- **Late Majority:** They adopt an innovation after the average participant. These individuals approach an innovation with a high degree of skepticism and after the majority of society has adopted the innovation. Late Majority are typically skeptical about an innovation, have below average social status, little financial liquidity, are in contact with others in the Late Majority and early majority and have little opinion leadership.

- **Laggards**: They are the last to adopt an innovation. Unlike some of the previous categories, individuals in this category show little to no opinion leadership. These individuals typically have an aversion to change-agents. Laggards typically tend to be focused on "traditions," have the lowest social status & lowest financial liquidity, are the oldest among adopters, and are in contact with only family and close friends.

The rise of transmedia Storytelling

Even the forms of storytelling and the thought used to create them has changed. Adapting to a system context, where each customer experience is different and personalized, where the audience presents expectations of consistency and contextualizes meaning, requires a resilience of content and stories, and an integrated and interconnected narrative in the conversation with the audience through every touch point, so they become transmedial.

Transmedia storytelling (also known as transmedia narrative or multi-platform storytelling) is the technique of a single story or story experience across multiple platforms and formats using current digital technologies, sequels, or adaptations, but usually working together with these other mediums.

From a production standpoint, transmedia storytelling involving creating content that engages an audience using various techniques to permeate their daily lives. In order to achieve this engagement, we will transmit multiple forms of media in order to deliver unique pieces of content in each channel. **Importantly, these pieces are not only linked together (overtly or subtly), but are in narrative synchronization with each other.**

According to **Matteo Stanzani** (transmedia director), the final end to creating a system of content, narratives, mystery, etc. is establishing not only a participative long-term relationship with the audience, but an audience centric journey of transformation or "pursuit of happiness."

According to **Jeff Gómez** (transmedia guru), there are three basic rules to transmedia storytelling:

1. **Your story needs to have some kind of aspirational quality.** It need to be meaningful. There's an upbeat quality to most successful trans media stories. It's got to be a story world you want to spend time in.

2. **You have to understand the media platforms** that you will have to handle and their language, **adapting your narrative** to these context.

3. **You need to think about and ultimately build an architecture for dialogue around** your transmedia implementation, and give your audience the ability to provide you feedback.

More Insights
(Search the following sentence in Google to retrieve the link)

- **Medium - The pursuit of happiness**
- **Indiwire - Three rules of transmedia storytelling**

Advertising to storytelling

The word Advertising today undoubtedly requires redefining. The context in which it was born and grew up, often combined with the creation and planning of campaigns in the form of billboards, banners, commercials, videos, buzz, etc. today, has changed. It remains despite an important element of a brand system in the context of the audience experience, but with different needs.

Advertising can no longer be an end in itself or to a single sales result or leads, just as it can no longer be coherent only with the brand's mission. Today it must also be consistent with the overall experience that the brand & business systems offers (and vice versa), increasing audience participation by releasing a perpetual or lasting value within the system.

And this is why more and more in the marketing and communications world, we are talking about Storytelling rather than Advertising, where the idea of building a constant, integrated narrative and evolving it with the system and its audience is better suited and produces better results in the brand's experience system.

More Insights
(Search the following sentence in Google to retrieve the link)

- AdWeek – Advertising isn't storytelling

- Why brands need to skip the Ads and start telling stories

- Campaign - Age doesn't matter - it's all about storytelling in advertising

Systematic activations as experiential ideas

Following the transmediality of storytelling, the activation of communications and content initiatives also must be reframed in an interconnected system context. As such, they assume all the typical characteristics of digital objects (ref: Digital Objects Architecture).

Activations need to satisfy these characteristics in order not to be isolated, but integrated into the brand's experience system and deliver real value to the audience. For those not familiar with the term "**Activation**" we could describe them as micro actions or **experiences** (pop-ups) related to specific communication campaigns or brand strategies.

Today these activations not only play a role in interacting differently with the audience, creating a deeper and more useful link, but also in producing content that's capable of becoming viral because of its authenticity.

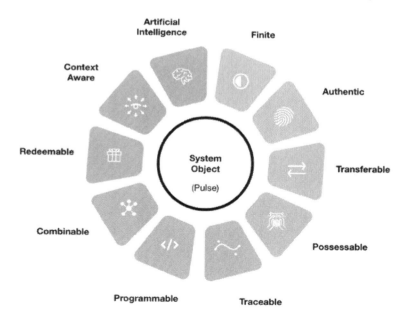

The rise of design as a way of thinking

Today the word "design" is increasingly mentioned in contexts not normally identified with the term, creating a lot of interpretative confusion due to different assumptions of the interlocutors. Today we talk about "Design Thinking" as a sort of method (or process) used to help teams realize complex, systematic and consistent intentions.

In other environments we talk about it to identify the decision protocol in working on transformative processes, organizing or developing products, services, business models and so on. Others still claim "Design Doing" as a true representative form of the Design world, where thinking is not enough, "you need to be able to do and realize."

The truth is that everyone is right. The term "design" today represents both a mindset, a process & protocol, but also an outcome and the method to achieve it.

Regarding "Design as a way of thinking" (as I prefer to define it so as not to confuse it with commercial terminologies), it has been talked about and studied for more than 70 years, a research and conversation that has always brought terms like human-centered, inclusion, holistic, sustainability and many others in the current conversations of marketing, business, strategies, etc. [2]

"Design as a way of thinking" moved out of the academic world at the beginning of the new millennium, when, thanks to the spread of the Internet, the growth of the system consciousness and the establishment of an experience economy structure, **Venture Capitals** and Investors realized that those businesses identified as "**New-Economy**," were able to scale and grow much more quickly and solidly than ever before.

The underlying cause lies in the fact that the economic and technological contexts represented fertile ground for business with a systematic approach focused on the distribution of experience solutions. In a short time we noticed how this cultural and methodological imprinting was made by the founders, normally Designers or Engineers who quickly passed from daily operations to the executive leadership of the company, bringing with it its strategic and **systematic culture**.

In support of these observations, many studies have validated the value of Design, as a way of thinking, in contexts such as Business, Organizational, Transformation, etc. One among them is a publication related to "**Design Thinking**" in a business context from **IDEO**. [1]

In a short time, **big brands have started to implement this culture in their own organizations**, developing new multidisciplinary design divisions including design as an aspect of thought and strategy, elevating it to leadership and often giving it a place in the C-suite. (ex: IBM, PepsiCo, Apple, CapitalOne, etc.) Other companies such as consulting, have seen a natural extension of their skills, giving life in the period of 2013-2017 to a real competition of **acquisitions of strategic design studios in the market**. [3]

Today, every **top business school in America includes Design Thinking programs**, as well as major **medical universities** and increasingly more colleges of different disciplines. In **China**, every Unicorn financed by VCs, includes at least one Designer among the founders and in the leadership. *[Source: John Maeda, Design in tech report 2018]*

Design today, becomes not only an outcome, not just a method or process, but also a strategic perspective that is increasingly important and necessary also in the world of Agencies to create value around the Brands both as an experience and as marketing.

For the first time Design disrupts organizations, demanding a more vertical than horizontal position, more strategic than executive, unfortunately creating confusion and friction within agencies. This forces more and more new generations feeling misunderstood to move initially in companies such as startups and now in brands, tech companies or consultancies.

[1] SOME POPULAR BOOKS ABOUT DESIGN IN CONTEXT AS BUSINESS

1.   Innovation by Design - Thomas Lockwood and Edgar Papke

2.   The Art of Innovation - Tom Kelly

3.   Design-driven Innovation - Roberto Verganti

4.   Change by Design - Tim Brown

5.   Customer-driven Transformation - Joe Heapy, Oliver King, James Samperi

6.   Rise of the DEO, Leadership by Design - Maria Giudice

7.   The pursuit of Absolute Engagement - Julie Littlechild

8.   Design Thinking for Strategic Innovation - Idris Mootee

9.   Design Innovation for the Built Environment - Michael Hensel

10.   Transformation - Roland Knauer

11.   Design Leadership -Raymond Turner

More Insights
(Search the following sentence in Google to retrieve the link)

- TechCrunch - Is the business school the new design school?

- TIME - The meaning of design Is up for debate. And that's a good thing

- John Maeda - Design in tech report 2018

- McKinsey - The business value of design

- Forbes - Why design thinking should also serve as a leadership philosophy

- Forbes - What is behind the rise of Chief Design Officer?

[2] SOME PEOPLE WHO HAVE CONTRIBUTED TO THE CONVERSATION
AROUND DESIGN AS A WAY OF THINKING

TODAY

Deborah Szebeko
Co-creation & Design

Ezio Manzini
Design & Inclusive

Tim Brown
Change by Design

David Kelly
Design Thinking for Business

Alistair Fuad-Luke
Design & Sustainability

Bill Moggridge
Design & Multidisciplinary

Ralf Faste
Design Thinking first time in a CV

Jane Fulton Suri
Design Ethics

Peter Rowe
"Design Thinking"

Liz Sanders
Tools, technics and methods on human-centered design

Nigel Cross
Design as a way of thinking in Education

Brian Lawson
Design as a way of thinking in Architecture

Donald Schön
The Reflective practitioner

Victor Papanek
Anthropology & Design

Robert McKim
Design as a way of thinking

Horst Rittel
Experience & Design

Herbert A. Simson
Design as a way of thinking

John Arnold
Human Centered

Buckminister Fuller
Cooperative Design

1958

47

[3] SOME OF THE ACQUISITIONS IN THE DESIGN BUSINESS BETWEEN 2014-2017

2004 - 2012

COMPANY	ACQUIRED BY
2004 Frog Design	Flextronics
2007 Doblin	Monitor
2009 Bigstock	Shutterstock
2010 TAT	Rim
2011 Sofa	Facebook
2011 Typekit	Adobe
2011 Method	Globallogic
2011 Helicopter	One Kings Lane
2012 Maaike	Google
2012 Bolt Peters	Facebook
2012 80/20	Square
2012 Cuban Council	Google
2012 Behance	Adobe

2013 - 2014

COMPANY	ACQUIRED BY	COMPANY	ACQUIRED BY
2013 Hot Studio	Facebook	2014 Cynergy Systems	KPMG
2013 Fjord	Accenture	2014 S&C	BCG
2013 Jet Cooper	Shopify	2014 Ultravisual	Flipboard
2013 Banyan Ranch	Deloitte	2014 Aviary	Adobe
2013 Hook & Loop	Infor		
2013 17FEET	Google		
2013 Hattery	Google		
2013 Mixel	Etsy		
2014 Carbon Design	Oculus/Facebook		
2014 Gecko Design	Google		
2014 Adaptive Path	Capital One		
2014 Reactive	Accenture		
2014 Flow Interactive	Deloitte		
2014 Optimal Experience	PWC		

2015

COMPANY	ACQUIRED BY
Teehan+Lax	Facebook
Spring Studio	BBVA
Lunar Design	McKinsey
Monsoon	Capital One
Designit	Wipro
Seren	Ernst & Young
Mobiento	Deloitte
Lapka	Airbnb
Catalyst	Cooper *consolidation
Akta	Salesforce
Chaotic Moon	Accenture
PacificLink	Accenture
Farm Design	Flex
Tactel	Panasonic Avionics
Fotolia	Adobe

2016

COMPANY	ACQUIRED BY	COMPANY	ACQUIRED BY
Slice of Lime	Pivotal	Carbon12	McKinsey
Resource/Ammirati	IBM	Mokriya	Nagarro
ecx.io	IBM	Uselab	Deloitte
Aperto	IBM	Tiny Hearts	Shopify
IDEO	Kyu Collective *minority	Boltmade	Shopify
Fahrenheit 212	Capgemini	VeryDay	McKinsey
Heat	Deloitte	Waybury	InVision
Gravitytank	Salesforce	Napkin	InVision
Fake Love	New York Times	Silver Flows	InVision
Karmarama	Accenture	Macaw	InVision
		Muzli	InVision

2017

COMPANY	ACQUIRED BY
Idean	Capgemini
Unity&Variety	Salesforce
Sequence	Salesforce

2018

COMPANY	ACQUIRED BY
Moment	Verizon

What it means to embrace design as a way of thinking

But what does it really mean to embrace Design as a way of thinking in an organization? Does it mean all of you become designers? Does it mean better planning? Does it mean becoming Agile? Or none of these?

To date, "Design Thinking" as it is sold, becomes an operative protocol with which to apply some principles of design thinking, in complex contexts to frame a problem and hypothesize a solution.

Design principles:

- **Holistic & systematic perspective:** The analysis of the problem must be done on tangible and intangible factors (**cause-effect**), including the impact of and in the context (**adoption strategy**) of the problem and of all the actors involved in the stage (**value of the system**).

- **Human centered perspective:** Understanding the perspective of your audience, not just as a consumer, but also as a person (**empathetic**). In an experience-stage, the audience behaves like an actor, going from being a consumer, to a user, to a guest, to a patient, etc. (**transformative & multidimensional role**) each of which assumes different needs and assumptions (**explicit and implicit handicaps**).

- **Visual evidence approach:** The understanding of complex and abstract problems is difficult for anyone, especially within a group of people, where different backgrounds, skillsets and assumptions generate different interpretations. The visualization of abstract elements such as ideas, processes, objects and their prototype not only allows human nature a more cognitive and profound comprehension (**understand**), but favors participating (**share**) by excluding misinterpretation and ease of dissemination (**influence**). The iconic representation of using a post-it wall and constructing objects with legos in design thinking workshops, plays the role of demonstrating the value of visual evidence.

- **Value of failure & aptitude for reframing:** The failure often derived from the observation of new perspectives following a prototype or other forms of visual evidence, is part of the design process as it always produces new knowledge (**learning**) and is often capable of unlocking a deadlock in the search for a solution (**reframing**). Therefore, failure is not only considered a value but also stimulates the opportunity to make this knowledge a useful (**discovery**) and competitive value (**monetizing**).

- **An unknown path to solutions:** Design thinking, like any other form of thought, becomes useful in contexts where the solution is not only unknown, but is found in unexplored spaces and directions. Therefore, an operative thought, a protocol in fact, becomes key to decide from time to time, which choice to make a step forward, between ambiguity and unclear perspectives (**process trust**), understanding new aspects, stimulating intuitions (**seeking patterns**), undertaking ideas or knowledge (**serendipity**) not considered before (**innovation context**).

Design community and design thinking controversy

The Design community is happy about how Design is raised to a more strategic point of view and the type of impact or value it can have on business, but at the same time it remains divided on the fact that "Design Thinking" remains only one side of the coin.

"Design Thinking is bullshit! Design is not a monster you 'unleash' to fix the world."

– **NATASHA JEN** *(Design Partner, Pentagram)*

–

"Design Thinking is being promoted everywhere these days.

Its success, along with the success of user-centered frameworks, is understandable. It is a simple, easy-to-understand system to develop concepts, articulate user needs and test ideas. Also, allowing non-designers to participate in the creative process.

On the other hand, it is removed, and by a long stretch, from the actual design skills that are necessary to deliver the products, brands and services that users will ultimately experience. So it's also understandable why a few classically trained designers are starting to react, calling it out as an over-simplistic approximation of the design process. Personally, I believe it's a matter of putting things in the right perspective.

A user-centric culture is beneficial to any business or organization, regardless of their design maturity, and this is where Design Thinking and a journey-based approach can really help (and I use a few of these tools in my design practice).

Beyond this, I do think that the design community should be more honest— the scope of Design Thinking is limited to strategic ideas and aspirational journeys—and even great ideas, if poorly executed, have very little or no value.

Successfully designing and executing ideas requires design resources, talent and expertise, that are much harder to find than design-thinkers or user-centered methodology practitioners.

So, today's trend of portraying Design Thinking as the ultimate value that design can bring to business is, not only deceiving, but could dangerously downplay other critical aspects of the design process.

In conclusion, I believe that Design Thinking could be a useful tool, but it has become important for the design community to put it in the right perspective."

– **ANDREA VARALLI** *(Executive Design Director)*

–

In the correct implementation of the Design practice, Design as a way of thinking and doing, they should be properly considered and integrated. After all, in the last decade we have seen many cases such as the value of design as a product or service, often generating a positive impact as a brand and a business, greater than any communication action, operational transformation and efficiency improvement.

Many today in fact discuss whether this spread of "Design Thinking" in business and marketing should only be called "System Thinking" and distinguish business that adopt a System-driven from a Design-Driven thinking.

More Insights
(Search the following sentence in Google to retrieve the link)

- Yes, design thinking Is bullshit...And We should promote it anyway

- Adobe - Design thinking is bullshit, Natasha Jen

Brand as an experience

It was **1998** when **Jospeh Pine II** and **Jim Gilmore** wrote an article for **Harvard Business Review** titled **"Welcome to the Experience Economy,"** explaining how more and more brands expressed themselves through experiences, creating stronger and lasting relationships with their audiences.

Human experiences are what we remember. Think about it. The best (and worst) experiences you had growing up, through your adult life are etched indelibly into your subconscious. Your first bike, the best party, that amazing summer holiday. This isn't brand waffle, this is science. This is how your brain actually works. Strong experiences create memories. From a business and company point of view, it's very straightforward. Delivering good experiences will keep your organization relevant and salient. Delivering bad experiences also makes you memorable, but in the wrong way.

At this time, however, the term "experiences" identifies isolated and independent activations around the brand itself, such as a pop-up shop or similar. Today, thanks to the impact of the Internet and the digital world of IoT, data, etc., the brand itself behaves and is received by the audience as a unique experience.

In an ever homogenized, codified, templated world, a unique brand 'Experience' is critical. Brands are defined by the experiences that they give. Adaption, loyalty, and advocacy are built on making people's lives genuinely better, easier, simpler.

Brand is experience, experience is brand. They are two parts that inform and support each other. 'Brand' sets the direction, answers the insight, and translates the business strategy into tangible actions. 'Experience' delivers it; shows us what 'sticks' and what doesn't; gives a company feedback, data, and measurement to course correct against; and ultimately lets the world decide if something is going to become part of our everyday culture or fail dead in the water.

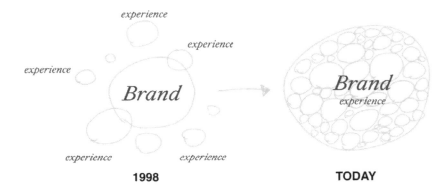

There's a big difference between the advertising model and the experience model in terms of making an authentic connection with your audience. It's relatively simple to get people to talk about you; it's much harder to get them to buy you. How can agencies find a role and a relation between advertising, communication, design and strategy in defining a brand and then adding value to its expression in the form of an experience?

If the expression of the brand takes place through an experience, it is perhaps time to contextualize the role of advertising, branding and marketing in a context of experience, linking the impact that every single action can have in the experience system, and then redefining the priorities for each brand and the skills needed to define tomorrow's agencies.

More Insights
(Search the following sentence in Google to retrieve the link)

- **CMO - Inside the living brand experience**

- **Forbes - Customer experience Is The New Brand**

- **HBR - Welcome in the experience economy**

Brand positioning in the experience economy

I asked positioning consultant **Marco De Veglia**, author of the "**Brand Positioning Formula**" to share his perspective on how brand positioning is changing in this economic context:

> With the evolution of branding from "communication" to "experience," how has this changed the effectiveness of a brand as a competitive tool? We have to answer this question first: What is a brand?
>
> In its most practical terms, a brand is a "shortcut to a problem's solution" that customers and businesses use in their relationship. So, the very role of a brand is to communicate that a problem is solved in a different - and for this reason, for this target, better - way than competitors.
>
> **Brand Positioning, or simply positioning, is the "mental model" that explains how this works:**
>
> 1. You understand what brands are in the customer mind and what ideas they communicate.
>
> 2. You find your differentiating Idea that makes your brand perceived as different and more interesting than competitors.
>
> 3. You communicate the differentiating Idea.
>
> Et voilà, you build an effective, competitive brand. (the original Brand Positioning Formula has a few more steps, but this is the essence of the process). Now, this process is evergreen because the way the mind works doesn't change.
>
> What changes is the way you do it. If today experience replaces communication in brand building, then the Brand Positioning Formula works with experience and not communication.

Experience becomes the benchmark for every step of the Brand Positioning Formula:

- You understand what brands are in the customer mind and for what experience ideas.

- You find your Differentiating Idea that makes your brand experience perceived as different and more interesting than competitors.

- You deliver the experience from the Differentiating Idea.

It is important this new brand paradigm of "brand as experience" can be managed in the framework of brand positioning. Because this makes the change in the brand building process, in terms of skills and tactics, definitely manageable and actionable.The positioning model still totally works in the experience economy. This doesn't mean things don't change. The change for agencies and brands is significative, as we have seen.

There is the need to understand "what is experience" and "how to use experience" to build and develop brands. This requires news skills, new people, new thinking and new organizations.

– **MARCO DE VEGLIA** *(Consultant)*

From Brand Positioning with advertising, to Brand Positioning with the experience.

More Insights
(Search the following sentence in Google to retrieve the link)

- **Amazon - Brand positioning formula, De Veglia, M. (2018)**

Design for a brand, not design a brand

"Your brand is what other people say about you when you're not in the room."

The quote in the title, by Jeff Bezos, Founder and CEO of Amazon, succinctly expresses the truth about branding. At its core, it's about personal connections and human emotions.

Maybe this can be a simplification of the meaning of the term, but it is enough to explain that the brand is the perspective of our audience, a perspective that we do not control, which perpetually changes and evolves and is influenced by many factors.

Therefore, we cannot design brands, but only design the context to create the conditions to generate or direct a brand in a specific direction.

In a context of system and experience economies, how do priorities change to transform or grow a brand by designing the conditions for which our audience changes its perspective organically, rather than imposing a new perspective on it?

More Insights
(Search the following sentence in Google to retrieve the link)

- **HBR - Alibaba focused build the ecosystem for e-commerce**

- **HBR - Design an ecosystem for "internet of things"**

Lead to balance: the negative space issue

Each of our initiatives is always aimed at the sole purpose of adding positive value to the brand. Brand, as an experience developed through a system, and as a system, will naturally balance the presence of a positive value with an equal negative value.

To better understand, think of **Airbnb**. As a platform to the real estate owners audience, it has created the opportunity to generate a new form of economic income through the short-term rent of its spaces (**positive value**). At the same time time in many residential areas the greater potential for profitability has triggered an increase in the cost of real estate (**negative value**).

In some **Airbnb** communities it has become a brand with a negative positioning more than a positive one, which has happened in some cases in **UBER** in some European cities.

In this respect, the preventive role of marketing & branding, through data, technologies, and exchange-value distribution, will play a key role in defining the future role of agencies.

More Insights
(Search the following sentence in Google to retrieve the link)

- **WSJ - How Airbnb affects home prices and rents**

Model, lead and feed a brand as an experience system

So let's try to dissect the "brand as an experience" not for traditional practices like advertising, social media, CRM, digital, etc., but from a system perspective, and what agencies can do to help a brand consolidate, grow and innovate. Each system must be analyzed at different altitudes, each of which builds the context for maximizing the effect of the others:

- **System to model:** Connect elements of the system in a meaningful way, by transforming, simplifying and creating a competitive advantage to track, understand, scale up faster & better, unlock opportunities and create conditions to innovate. This part of the agencies' work is a long-term and integrated relationship with the brand led by a design multidisciplinary & inclusive perspective.

- **System to lead:** Organize, plan and create value in the system though forms of interaction between all the participants to leverage organic activities, create opportunities, adapt to the changes and create the condition to grow. This part of the agencies' work is a mid-term and collaborative relationship with the brand led by a strategic multidisciplinary and inclusive perspective.

- **System to feed:** Tell stories (storytelling) and deploy ideas able to keep the system alive through forms of communication, experiential activations and dialog with the participants to create the conditions to increase activities and move audiences into and through the system. This part of the agencies' work is a short-term and incremental relationship with the brand, led by a creative multidisciplinary and inclusive perspective.

BRAND AS AN EXPERIENCE SYSTEM

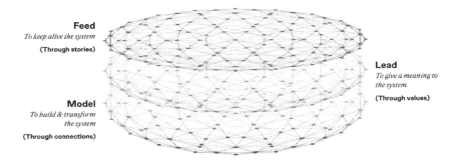

Feed
To keep alive the system
(Through stories)

Lead
To give a meaning to the system.
(Through values)

Model
To build & transform the system
(Through connections)

Why is this approach important?

It is important because it changes the way to prioritize what is relevant to add value to the brand as an experience and which KPIs are used to measure the results.

As you might have noticed, what leads in these three altitudes of observation, are not skills or a specific practice as Visual Design, Technology, or Planning, but mindsets (or a way of thinking), such as Design, Strategy and Creativity.

What kind of agency do you want to be? To feed, to lead or operate at any level of the system?

More Insights
(Search the following sentence in Google to retrieve the link)

- **Business Insider – Consumers are doing everything they can to avoid ads. Here's how P&G, one of the world's largest advertisers, is finding a way around that**

Brand building blocks

But how is the brand perceived, as an experience, from an audience point of view? As we have already discussed, brands today are not only judged by what they do and say, but also by how they do it, in a holistic way and from an audience perspective (experience).

The perception by the audience takes place in a completely different and vertical way in the experience system. Based on my experience, I have identified seven building blocks, divided into three groups of platforms:

- **Facing Platform Set:** All these factors, organized as Identity and Conversational platforms, are the audience-facing elements, traditionally identified within the world of communication, advertising, branding & marketing.

- **Configuration Platform Set:** Factors in the configuration group include aspects of Exchange Value and Interactions. Normally these factors are not attributable to explicit elements but remain highly tangible in the audience experience. Normally identified within the world of strategic design, experience design, marketing, partnerships, community governance, loyalty programs & CRM.

- **Delivery Platform Set:** Last but not least, if hidden from the audience perspective, the Technology, Business and Organization groups remain tangible factors. All these factors in a context of experience, have a dramatic impact on the distribution of value in the brand, determining and influencing the other groups, in terms of resilience, scalability and stimulation of innovation contexts. Normally these factors are identified with skills that are only recently embraced by the agency world, and in some cases still in the adoption phase, such as technology & data, sustainability, business & brand consulting, employees' experience, working models and digital & business transformation.

BUILDING BLOCKS
(Last update January 2019)

SYSTEM	FACING SET	
Brand	› Identity › Conversational	Explicit and tangible factors
	CONFIGURATION SET	
	› Exchange value › Interaction	Implicit and tangible factors
	DELIVERY SET	
	› Technology › Business › Organization	Hidden and tangible factors

Marketing & brands: new sets of KPIs

In this change of perspective the meaning of what the brand is, even the way the results of marketing actions are identified, can no longer be the same.

The experience is evaluated not only by the number of participants involved, but also by the intensity of the participation itself. Consequently, the success factors of marketing, advertising, communication, etc. should be related only to the participation aspect.

Now let us consider participation and business as two wheels (or toothed gears) of different but connected scales. Where the speed of participation is greater, the greater the thrust the business receives, increasing in turn the speed (growth).

What are the metrics that marketing can use today to measure the impact on participation? And which system should be used to connect participation with the impact in the business wheel? What is a minimum increase that can be considered sustainable and which is not? A whole new form of marketing **KPIs** must be redefined and standardized in today's context..

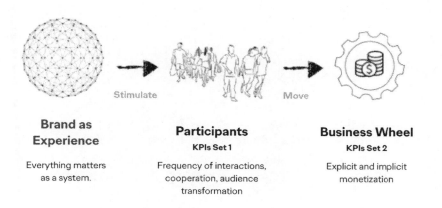

Brand as Experience	Participants	Business Wheel
	KPIs Set 1	KPIs Set 2
Everything matters as a system.	Frequency of interactions, cooperation, audience transformation	Explicit and implicit monetization

Brand experience equity

Today, more than ever, it has become crucial for each brand to understand and monitor its **Brand Experience Equity (BXQ)**, in order to contextualize the impact that every marketing, communication, branding or strategy action has. The BXQ thus represents the new index of the value that the experience system of each brand provides to its audience, much more than the traditional Brand Equity.

If the **Brand Equity** resides in the consumer's awareness of the characteristics of the brand, the value and its associations, guiding the attribution of a perception, the **Brand Experience Equity** becomes more inclusive and empathetic with the public, defining rather an attribute of affiliation and membership.

In this perspective, the BXQ is not only appreciated through economic growth, market share and prestige, but also in aspects of **innovation** and predisposition for an **exponential growth**.

Every single operation of marketing, communication, activations, technology or implementations of innovative solutions, should be evaluated not only in a **ROI** or **Leads** generated context but also in terms of **BXQ**, through a system perspective **necessary in the construction of experience stages.**

If a **communications operation**, **campaign** or **marketing** action can produce 3 million Viewers or Leads, but doesn't increase your BXQ, can we consider these results a success or not?

Suppose also in the short term these results also translate into a fair economic increase in sales, remember, **that the BXQ represents a stronger and deeper relationship with its audience** and that requires a **medium-long period of time to change**, contrary to the perception of a brand, which is much more volatile because it is more superficial.

In this case, in the face of a fair and immediate ROI, we should anticipate a loss of participation that could project for a long time, reducing economic growth significantly and requiring new and greater strategic investments.

Memo

Experience from the infinite journeys through a system.

–

Systematic ideas and solutions require a systematic method, approach and mindset.

–

A system to model, to lead and to feed.

–

Grow the experience system to grow participation and business revenues.

Agencies

–

The journey of the phoenix. A perspective shift.

The long path of the agencies

In the '70s, due to a massive and constant emigration from the Caribbean and South America, the American record industry saw in Latin American music a potential to be commercially exploited.

A cultural and musical heritage made up of different rhythms and styles: Timba, Guaguancó, Bomba, Cumbia, Rumba, Pachanga, Mambo, Guajira, and many others.

Too many kinds to be marketed to the masses and too much effort needed to promote their presence in radios and shops. So the record industry decided to label them all under one name and genre: Salsa.

The term 'Agency' today can be compared to the term 'Salsa,' for the function of representing different forms of interpretation under the same umbrella such as: **Advertising, Marketing, Brand** and recently **Digital** and **Experience**.

These are all terms that the exponential technological innovation of the last 20 years has transformed and redefined, in many cases blurring the differences, leading to the creation of often multidisciplinary realities defined as *integrated* or *360*.

Each agency has its own DNA of skills, methods, processes and narratives, as well as its own business and client size, often creating confusion in the general public, in terms of expectations and/or interpretation of its role.

In the last ten years the world of agencies has not only faced an identity and growth crisis, caused by the downsizing and fragmentation of the media system and the impact that the Digital world has had on changing the dynamics of communication and marketing, but also from the increasingly strong presence of tech companies first and consultants now, in the budget traditionally allocated to the world of the agencies themselves.

The effects were many and varied, from the downsizing of some realities, to the merging of others in an attempt to consolidate the business and redefine their skills, until undertaking a radical operational transformation, looking for a new identity, a new role in the market.

A role that fundamentally does not change the ultimate goal of any form of agency that is to create and give value around brands, but that more and more redefines a new way to do it.

The friction of a successful heritage

For decades the Agencies represented a model of success, capable of sustaining operations with large margins of net profit and consequently able to invest and innovate.

A bit like "**Virgilio**," a character who guided **Dante** of the **Divine Comedy**, the agencies were able to guide the brands through the complex media system, understand its rules, increase market share, save brands from problematic situations and define the success of many others.

Agencies for a long time had the keys to comprehending the market, the brand and consumers; and to decoding the link and the effect on business growth.

A noble, impeccable legacy, made up of big names, great people and brilliant ideas that have marked the history of many companies and the culture of this business.

But the world has changed, technology has and is changing the way of doing business with a speed never seen before. The consumers themselves have changed, with much more diversity, with many more economic dynamics, creating an increase in opportunities but also more challenges.

New players were born and grew up in this scenario, defining new rules, new dynamics and a new culture around the link between the interaction with consumers and the economic growth of brands, questioning the whole old creed of that world called Advertising & Marketing.

The agencies were not blind, they saw the change coming, but changing and transforming is always a difficult, expensive and unknown process.

Change does not mean buying skills through acquisitions of companies or exotic talent. Changing does not mean presenting itself differently and offering new services.

Transforming means changing one's way of thinking, as well as the perspective with which one faces and creates solutions to challenges; changing the way of working, organizing the company and how it relates to the outside world.

Innovating today is not what you do or why you do it, but how you do it.

The excessive success and importance of a great culture generated over decades by the agencies themselves, was the real problem of their lack of transformation: **"Too big to change."**

THE MULTIVERSE OF THE AGENCIES

The agency world is also affected by what the information world today calls the **Bubble Effect**. The presence of these information systems around us, which shows us what we want and what we believe is useful, often also plays the role of making us ignore other realities or perspectives. **Sir Martin Sorrell** mentioned this phenomenon following an interview last October:

"The biggest impediment on the world of agencies in innovating is the bubble effect in which they live, ignoring in fact the presence of other operational methods, other forms of business to do marketing or advertising."

– **SIR MARTIN SORRELL** (Former CEO of WPP Holding)
Ignition 2018

An unsustainable model

For decades, the organizational model of large agencies has grown around the large advertising and marketing budgets that each brand allocates from year to year managing its distribution through one or more agencies, which are involved in developing initiatives, content and planning for what was called the "media system."

The "**Agency of Records–#AOR**" represented for a long time the final phase of every relationship between an agency and a brand, an unofficial acknowledgment of continuous and undisputed collaboration, which allowed the agencies to invest in talent, experimentation, support and business development activities. This stable and long-term relationship planning made it possible to construct its structures in the likeness of its clients in order to facilitate their interaction and integration.

It was clear already at the beginning of 2000 to the community developing around the new economy, that digital would become the new reference system, incorporating the old media system, and that large agencies, especially integrated ones, were increasingly giants with feet of clay or "walking dead" in some cases.

This is because with the development of the digital world and the so-called New Economy, big brands noticed how the ROI of advertising budgets no longer justified such investments, and a more democratic access to the digital system allowed the brands themselves to be able to build their own system, integrate it with others and directly manage the relationship with their audience.

The budgets began not to be decommissioned, but to be moved to other forms of investment, diversified in technology, content production, social & audience governance, experience, etc.

The large **Agencies** and **Ad holding companies**, to maintain not only their dominant position in relation to the big brands, but also the control of those budgets capable of maintaining their structure, started buying companies/skills such as those mentioned above and thus extended on what they already did in the digital world without any distinction.

Engagement with its audience began to derive from forms other than traditional advertising, and the impact on the brand often took place from a technology and/or a service of the company itself, rather than from an advertising campaign.

And it is in this period (2000-2005) that new forms of "agencies," based on new operational models, began to grow, some to the point of turning into real global networks like **R/GA** and subsequently seeing consulting firms, such as Accenture and Deloitte, trespassing in the digital marketing world.

Let us remember that **R/GA** was born as a Production Studio, and arrived at the big table with projects such as **IBM**'s global website, **Nokia** Vine and **Nike**+.

In addition to this fragmentation, the new economy, has shifted entire budgets of the media centers, directly into **Google**, **Amazon**, **Facebook** and **Apple**, creating in turn the various internal Agencies, thus consolidating an exclusive relationship with the brand without intermediaries.

In recent years (2014-2018) two out of three talent have moved from an agency to a tech or consulting company.

The traditional media system was no longer the dominant system, but it had become one of the many systems, within what some called the system of systems ("digital").

The organizational model of the Agencies was no longer sustainable economically because fewer and fewer companies were investing in an AOR. Increasingly, the retainer model was migrating to an on-demand model and as a result the available budgets were reduced.

A mix of deadly complications: a complex organization, a cultural friction, a fragmented business, a budget dispersion, have shown how a new operational and business model for the world of agencies was and still is necessary.

ONE-YEAR STOCK PERFORMANCE OF MAJOR AD COMPANIES (2017-2018)

More Insights
(Search the following sentence in Google to retrieve the link)

- **AdWeek – Agencies, why the traditional agency model is struggling to keep up with demand**

- **Financial Times – Advertising companies struggle to adapt to a new world.**

- **Forbes - The State of advertising has never been worse**

CONSULTANCIES ARE GROWING THEIR BUSINESS BY 4-6% IN 2017
Agencies retract by 10-20% in the same period.
Source: GartnerL2

Decrease of salary due a
juniorization of resources   Struggling to survive   Growth and diversification

Agencies are facing as well a juniorization of their talents due to cost-cutting strategies.

NUMBER OF EMPLOYEES NEEDED IN 2017
Source: GartnerL2

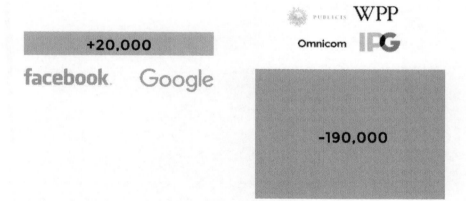

Common weakness: the CMOs

Another strong brake on the transformation of the agencies is a problem shared with many brands and by the **Chief Marketing Officers.**

In a world where the market no longer buys the product or service, but the experience and value that comes from it; a world where consumers are increasingly linked to the experiences that the brand itself, even CMOs have had to face this new challenge from an operational point of view.

Every idea, every project today, is no longer only linked to communication aspects, but increasingly impacts vertically on the entire company. More and more the product, service, distribution, and organization of the company become key factors in every operation, creating an interference of skills between different executives, very often 'not in charge' for certain choices and changes in a short period.

All this often turns into complicated internal policies that lead to stalemate situations or misalignment of competencies, impacting the permanence of CMOs and consequently the relationship with the agencies.

In fact, this dependence of the agencies' world on CMOs has increasingly turned into the real weak point of the business generation.

Today the agencies, through the creation of the division of consulting, data and design are increasingly looking for new points of contact with the brands, often independent of the CMOs themselves.

While CMOs, in the more traditional interpretation of their role, increasingly become rare animals, new figures in organizations begin to replace them, facing their mission under a complete and different perspective.

The **Chief Experience Officer**[1] (CXO) thus becomes the new orchestrator of the company's brand, to which marketing reports.

AVG. TENURE OF CMOS IN A COMPANY
Source: Harvard Business Review

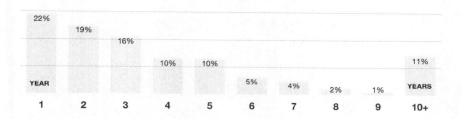

"Most Chief Marketing Officers have not been in their positions long. More than 40% have been in their roles two years or less, and 57% have been in them three years or less. CMOs find barriers and friction, often don't have enough experience to handle internal dynamics or they cannot find the right partners inside the company to help their work in this change."

– HARVARD BUSINESS REVIEW *(June 2017)*

In other cases, due to the complexity and size of the business, the role of the **CXO** is replaced by figures such as the **Chief Growth Officer** (CGO) and the **Chief Design Officer** (CDO), where the former focuses on identifying gaps and opportunities to feed the system experience and consolidate it, while the second is focused on building and transforming the experience system in order to scale up and innovate it. (es: PepsiCo, Apple)

In all these cases, **traditional marketing units report to these roles.**

This new, powerful combination of multidisciplinary and authorized change-maker roles represents the best approach to front this new age of business challenges made by a complex system of interaction with the consumers, where sharing data allows for tailoring experiences to each consumer and provides a valuable exchange value across any touch point of the brand/business ecosystem at any time.

–

"Design has become a perspective playing a key role in the experience economy."

– HARVARD BUSINESS REVIEW *(2018)*

–

"So why is design making the move into the C-suite? Similar to the birth of title Chief Marketing Officer (CMO) role in the early 1990s when companies were seeking to differentiate and strengthen their brands through creative marketing leadership, the shift in the last decade has been towards design."

– FORBES *(2015)*

–

"From CMOs to CXOs: Experience is the North Star that guides everything that marketers do and understand through the lens of the consumer."

– THE DRUMS *(2016)*

"Legacy brands including Mastercard and MetLife to Marriott are responding to the threat by appointing chief experience officers to build closer relationships with customers."

– BUSINESS INSIDER *(2019)*

[1] Unfortunately the meaning of "Experience" in many business contexts refers to the traditional UX field. In many cases the hundreds of Chief Experience Officers hired in the latest years in different companies are merely product or service designers and very few of them are truly CXOs in a more holistic approach including business and brand context.

More Insights
(Search the following sentence in Google to retrieve the link)

- **AdAge - CMOs struggle to acclimate to changing landscape**

- **HBR - The trouble with the CMOs**

- **DTC brands are shaking up retail by providing great customer experience**

The growth of consultancies vs agencies

The Consultants now compete with the Agencies in a blurry space between Marketing, Experience & Innovation where a large amount of money is moving.

Companies such as **Accenture Interactive**, **Deloitte Digital**, **Cognizant Interactive**, **IBM iX**, **PwC Digital Service** and **CapGemini** (to name a few) today are increasingly becoming the new "AOR" and as partners of strategic companies who want a more direct way to interact with customers, with a focus on the customer experience. On the other side, Ad Holdings and Big Agencies create their consulting skills, in order to establish new forms of relationships with their customers.

This is because, in the context of the experience economy, **both Agencies and Consultants operate on the company system**, a system that, from the consumers' perspective is called Brand, from the operational perspective is called Business.

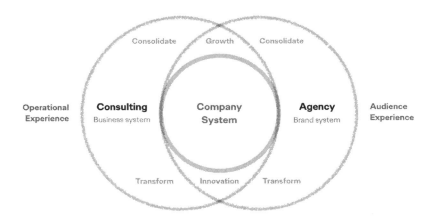

Both perspectives try to transform the system, optimize it, identify gaps, opportunities and innovate it; for both, everything has a role, everything has a relevance for the ultimate purpose of making it grow in economic terms.

Contrary to the perception that the two worlds converge, the world of Agencies and that of Consultants act with very different assumptions, methods and goals, but operate on the same system, a system with the same rules and needs of skills. **"Who leads the system, owns the business."** It thus becomes clear that more and more overlaps between the two worlds become frequent, even if Agencies and Consulting Firms remain very different from each other in the thought and the value that they can produce.

[1] M&A SPENDING OF CONSULTING FIRM AND ADVERTISING AGENCIES 2018 ($/MILLION)
Last updated Sept 2018

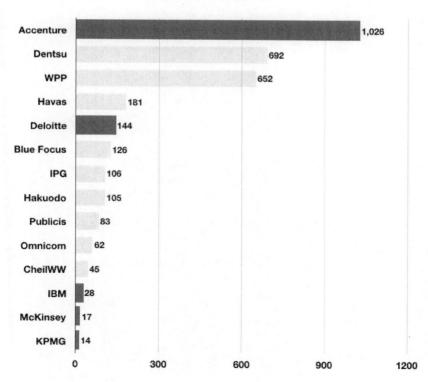

[2] CONSULTING INTEREST AND INVESTMENTS WITH A SYSTEM PERSPECTIVE IN THE LATEST DECADE

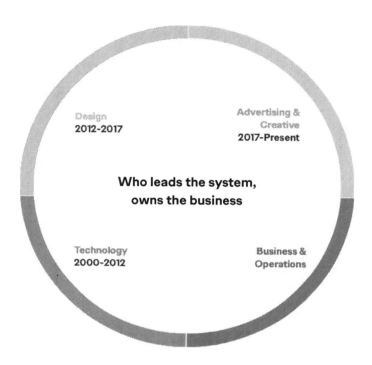

More Insights
(Search the following sentence in Google to retrieve the link)

- **Forbes - Why the consultancies won't replace ad agencies anytime soon**

- **AdAge - The rise is on! How IBM, Accenture, PwC and Deloitte Are Shaking Up the marketing Industry**

- **Consultancy UK - Accenture, Deloitte and McKinsey spent $1.2 billion on agency acquisitions**

The ambitions of emerging business in technology and design

Thanks to the explosion of the new economy responsible for developing new business models linked to the existence of an experience economy model, practices such as Design and Technology, have acquired a new meaning and value, elevating their aspirations.

A new business narrative has been written, a new way of measuring its value has been calculated, and a new method to evaluate its impact on business and brand systems has been learned to use.

In the experience economy, consumers no longer judge brands only for what they do and say, but also how they do it and integrate themselves with other systems.

And that's why, first the consulting companies like **Accenture**, **Deloitte** and **McKinsey** and then big brands like **IBM**, **Amazon**, **Apple**, **PepsiCo**, **CapitalOne** (just to name a few), have built or inserted in their strategic core-business, both the prospect of technology and design.

Today at the table of the C-Suite and leadership of companies, we no longer speak only of economic aspects or presence in the market, but also of technology and design, with an equivalent decision-making power with other perspectives.

1. Harvard Business Review (Leverage Design Thinking for company management, 2018)

2. Ginni Rometty, IBM CEO (Moved the Design perspective into the leadership in the 2014)

3. Indra Nooyi, PepsiCo CEO (Hired the first Chief Design Officer in charge for all brand experience in 2012)

4. Stanford University (All top business schools in US have a Design program)

More Insights
(Search the following sentence in Google to retrieve the link)

- **The Conversation - Why designers have arrived in corporate boardrooms**

- **CNBC - Designers rise to top jobs as companies rethink how to inspire the consumer**

- **Quartz - Why are we still arguing for the business value of design? (Good design is good business)**

Creative & marketing strategy leads, everybody else executes

In agencies we are witnessing a generational and cultural shift that increasingly becomes a source of internal and managerial frictions.

More and more often, talent spend a lot more time on project teams defending their perspectives (as a practice), instead of spending their energies on defending the agency's perspective on the client. In particular in the last 10 years this has increased the perception that the big agencies were no longer an ideal environment for those who wanted to work in the practices of **Design**, **Technology** and **Data**.

This is because in the old model of the creative world, the "Creatives" (Directors, Executive and Chief Executive) have always been the supreme guide to every project, where every other practice and competence had an almost executive, rather than a strategic, role.

On the other hand, the new generations, especially those formed in the field of Design, Technology or Experience, are aware of the value they can give and carry with them an expectation that is often very different from the operating context that is often found in an agency.

Just consider how many design schools today include more and more business design, design management and strategic design programs.

This is a problem that requires a new type of leadership that can establish a new operational model. In 2018 alone, many big agencies such as **Ogilvy**, **McCann**, **Droga5** and **CP-B** have lost their Global CCO and many are wondering if this role is no longer relevant to the needs of the market. (last updated December 2018).

1. IBM Institute report: The modern marketing mandate (How Chief Marketing Officers are transforming into Chief Experience Officers.)

2. Book: Rise of the DEO, Leadership by Design

3. Book: Customer-Driven Transformation: How being Design-led helps companies get right services to market.

More Insights
(Search the following sentence in Google to retrieve the link)

- **AdWeek - The death of the global chief creative officer**

- **Linkedin - Are we facing a talent exodus from creative agencies?**

- **DigiDay - UK media agencies are facing a leadership crisis**

- **FastCompany - These companies are vacuuming up everybody else's tech talent**

The fragmented offer and the challenge to measure the value

In all this divergence and diversification of the market, the next problem for the agencies was the validation of ideas and measuring their value. How do they validate tactics that not only involve communication ideas, but also the development and transformation of services, especially when these have an impact on how a company operates and manages a given business?

A new form of **KPIs** and index factors are emerging; a new way of connecting activities to the brand and business growth is forming.

Data competence increasingly becomes a strategic key in the world of creativity, but at the same time, the use of inclusive, participatory and collaborative methods with its customers becomes the order of the day, as they are indispensable in the learning process and the alignment of the brand and agency in the validation of ideas.

In all this, the consultative method will play an ever-increasing role in agencies.

More Insights
(Search the following sentence in Google to retrieve the link)

- **McKinsey - The business value of design**

- **Forbes - Telling more compelling stories through design thinking**

- **Forbes - Great customer experience is the combination of design thinking and agile marketing**

- **AdWeek - Infographic how design thinking is affecting the workplace improving customer experience and getting results for brands**

1. McKinsey: The Business Value of Design

2. Forrester: The Total Economic Impact of IBM's Design Thinking practice

3. Book: The Art of Innovation.

A double speed business: who falls & who rises

Is the entire "advertising & marketing" industry struggling? No. Only the big organizations are suffering for a lack of opportunities to adapt in the past, and change quickly now.

But in the market, hundreds of small-medium agencies, born in the latest 10-15 years, are successfully growing, more often acquiring market share and often big client accounts or investments (ex: **MediaMonks**, **R/GA**, **AKQA** and more).

Many justify this phenomenon almost exclusively for a factor of greater financial flexibility, such as lower structural costs, more manageable projects, smaller customers and an openness to experimentation, investment and risk with a consequence of greater creativity.

In reality there are also other factors that differentiate these new and growing structures from others. Excluding for a moment those who produce content or tools that in this case we should identify as "**studios**," in the market we can identify two types of young agencies: the first that specializes in a **vertical perspective** of the brand's experiences (eg: Identity, Conversational, Technology, etc.); the second one is focused on a **horizontal perspective** on a system-level experience (adding value by Model, Lead or Feed).

In both these cases, these realities also grow due to a **systematic mindset**, a more **multidisciplinary and inclusive** organization with a leadership grown in an experience economy context that is able to establish new forms of **business narratives** and **validate ideas** with their own customers.

In short, the cost factor plays an important part, but the real competitive and differentiating advantage remains the operational model that these organizations are based on.

More Insights
(Search the following sentence in Google to retrieve the link)

- **Forrester - Midsize digital agencies = experience success**

Experience economy and the future role of the agencies

What kind of agency will survive and evolve in the near future? Doing what and how? An agency more like a consulting firm, or a consultancy increasingly similar to the agencies? **Will the agencies be acquired by consulting companies, incorporated into the brands themselves or reduced to specialized studios?**

These, and many others, are the increasingly frequent questions of those who observe and work in this business.

The future is not so much in what we would do and how we would do it, but why we do it. It does not matter if the agency, like a modern **Millennium Falcon**, will operate in one or more building blocks of the brand as an experience, or if it will be more similar to an **Imperial Star Wars Spaceship** operating on one or more levels of the brand's system.

What will determine the growth, the ability to innovate, to guide the brand's system of its customers (and consequently own the business), will be the ability to operate with a systematic mindset, establishing an organizational and operational model capable of removing silos (multidisciplinary and inclusive*), careful to produce and distribute value in the brand through all the platforms that constitute the perspective of its audience, integrating, operating and balancing the whole system.

Advertising and marketing will gain a new meaning, emerging from different skills, changing the roles of leadership in companies, and transforming the way to work and build relationships with their customers.

A capacity that must not only reside in a new form of leadership, but in the entire organizational and operational structure, from how we think about the brand to what role it has in the socio-economic context in which we live.

We need a vision capable of inoculating new ways of thinking, supporting individual talent to participate and contribute to the cohesion of the whole structure by developing a new way of working and forging teams with a new mindset.

It is necessary to find a **new way to measure** the results of what is done in the brand and marketing world, especially in an experience economy context, **where the participation and interaction of the audience has a direct impact on the business wheel.**

The real transformation of the agencies must take place starting from a new organizational model, a model capable of embracing a systematic, inclusive and multidisciplinary perspective starting from the leadership to the single talent in a cohesive manner.

A systematic model, for systematic solutions; a model that defines a structure's rules but not the ultimate structure. A model capable of creating the conditions for a persistent transformation and an exponential form of innovation.

*=Inclusion as mindset, perspective of problem solving, skillset and organization-level..

Memo

Making brands matter means making experience matter.

–

Design & consultative perspectives must sit at the business table next to strategy and creative.

–

CMOs are no longer the only face of the client

Assessment

—

Self assessment

Brand platforms

How does it work?

- **As an Agency**: Self assess in which sets, platforms and factors your agencies can provide help to the brand experience from an audience perspective. With this assessment you will be able to identify opportunities and gaps in your business offer, organization and relationship with clients.

- **As a Brand:** Use this assessment to understand in which sets, platforms and factors you are investing in brand experience from an audience perspective. Ask your agency (in-house or external) and partners to do the same exercise in order to understand how they can help you.

- **How do you calculate your platform score?**
  Multiply the number of checked items by 5 and divide the results by the total items available. [**Score** = (checked items x 5) / total items]

EX: If you are a traditional advertising creative agency, and you mostly produce video commercials and campaigns you should check all that is in the Conversation platform (Storytelling model, Storytelling content). If you are a Marketing Agency, probably you will check elements in the Facing and the Configuration sets. If you are a Digital Agency you will probably check elements between the Configuration and Delivery sets.

Facing Set		Configuration Set		Delivery Set		
Identity	**Conversation**	**Exchange Value**	**Interaction**	**Technology**	**Business**	**Organization**
Common practices: (9)	Elements: (10)	Elements: (8)	Elements: (10)	Elements: (8)	Elements: (12)	Elements: (8)
▨ Visual identity system	▨ Language system	▨ Commercial incentives	▨ Stores experiences	▨ Open data	▨ Distribution	▨ Knowledge management
▨ Brand visual extensions	▨ Storytelling model	▨ Experience incentives	▨ Digital channels	▨ Data learning	▨ On demand model	▨ Decentralization and talent empowerment
▨ Environmental sensitivity	▨ Content model	▨ Loyalty model	▨ Cross-Selling tactics	▨ Data prediction	▨ Subscriptions model	▨ Employees experience
▨ Mission	▨ Personalization system	▨ User-flow value	▨ Diversifications tactics	▨ Platforms integration	▨ Sustainability	▨ Processes value
▨ Experience ethics rules	▨ Artificial intelligence	▨ Customer-flow value	▨ Experience integration	▨ Technology & marketing automation	▨ Token policy	▨ Inclusion
▨ Value alignment	▨ Employees playbooks	▨ Co-branding operations	▨ Experience activations	▨ Emerging technologies adoption	▨ R&D	▨ Working model
▨ Experience value	▨ Curation	▨ Value to the experience	▨ Experience simplification	▨ Technology ecosystem transparencies	▨ Partners experience	▨ Data accessibility
▨ Brand experience rule	▨ Customer care system	▨ Value from the experience	▨ Experience automation	▨ Data security	▨ Monetization models	▨ Transparency
	▨ Crowdsourcing		▨ Experience enabling		▨ Digital payments	
	▨ Community dialog & Social reputation		▨ Community system		▨ Consumer financial platforms	
					▨ Risk sharing	
					▨ Licensing	
Score ___	Score ___	Score ___	Score ___	Score ___	Score ___	Score ___

Facing Set

Identity

Common practices: (9)

- Visual Identity system
- Brand visual extensions
- Brand UI system
- Environmental sensitivity
- Mission
- Experience ethics rules
- Values alignment
- Experience value
- Brand experience role

Score ___

Conversation

Elements: (10)

- Language system
- Storytelling model
- Content model
- Personalization system
- Artificial intelligence
- Employee playbooks
- Curation
- Customer care system
- Crowdsourcing
- Community dialog & Social reputation

Score ___

Configuration Set

Exchange Value

Elements: (9)

- Economics incentives
- Experience incentives
- Loyalty model
- User-flow value
- Customer-flow value
- Data privacy
- Co-branding operations
- Value in the experience
- Value from the experience

Score ___

Interaction

Elements: (10)

- Stores experience
- Digital channels
- Cross Selling tactics
- Diversifications tactics
- Experience integration
- Experience activations
- Experience simplification
- Experience automation
- Experience enabling
- Community system

Score ___

Delivery Set

Technology

Elements: (8)

- Open data
- Data learning
- Predictive analysis
- Platforms integrations
- Technology & marketing automation
- Emerging technologies adoption
- Technology ecosystem transparencies
- Data security

Score ___

Business

Elements: (12)

- Distribution
- On-demand model
- Subscriptions model
- Sustainability
- Token policy
- R&D
- Partners experience
- Monetization models
- Digital payments
- Consumer financial platform
- Risk sharing
- Licensing

Score ___

Organization

Elements: (8)

- Knowledge management
- Decentralization and talent empowerment
- Employee experience
- Processes value
- Inclusion
- Working model
- Data accessibility
- Transparency

Score ___

Agency fingerprint

Try to project your platform's capabilities through the system perspective

Note: If you checked Loyalty Model (Exchange Value platform) because you help brands with their loyalty programs, and you can provide only communication, governance and defining the type of rewards, but you are not capable (or in charge) of defining and deploying the rewarding metrics system and tools, your capability will be only in the FEED and LEAD layer and not in the DESIGN layer.

SAMPLE

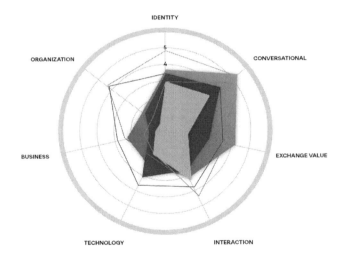

Average Marketing Agency

Solid areas: competencies / expertise
Lined areas: opportunities for growth.

TO FEED

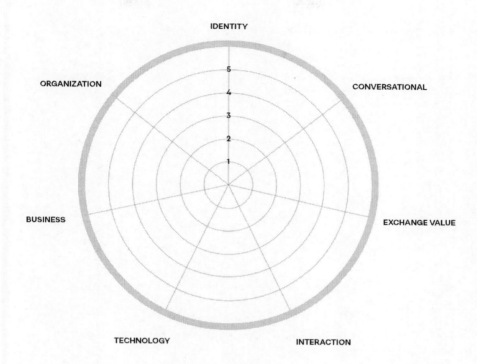

Common client-side partners
CMOs & Product Leaders

From a perspective of feeding by content, ideas, activations and communications for the systems

TO LEAD

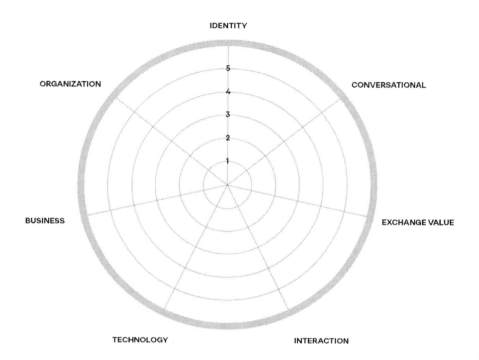

Common client-side partners
CMOs, CIOs, CGO CTOs & Products Leaders

From a perspective of organizing, planning, creating value, system governance and other tasks.

TO MODEL

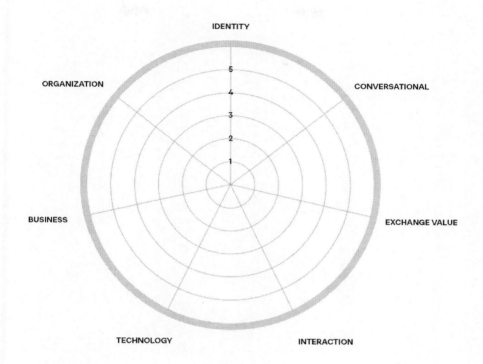

Common client-side partners
CEO, COO, CMOs, CIOs, CGO, CTOs & Product Leaders

From a perspective of designing, changing, transforming & building systems.

BLUEPRINT

A new type of leadership

–

Resilient: how can you lead an organization in a continuous and transformative economy experience stage?

A system oriented & multidisciplinary mindset

Like the new organizational model of teams from a system perspective, the new leadership must also have or acquire this type of mindset.

Despite their desire to disrupt and take risks, the **new leaders must be system thinkers** who understand the interconnectedness of their world. They know that each part of their organization overlaps and influences one another. They know unseen connections surround what's visible. This helps to give their disruptions intended, rather than chaotic, impact and makes their risk-taking more conscious.

The new leadership isn't troubled by change. In fact, they openly promote and encourage it. They understand traditional approaches, but are not dominated by them. As a result, they are comfortable disrupting the status quo if it stands in the way of their dream. They try to think and act differently than others. They recognize this ability as a competitive advantage.

Leadership with a mindset focused on a system perspective is intuitive, either by nature or through experience. They have the ability to feel what's right by using their intense perceptual and observational skills or through deep expertise (pattern seekers). This doesn't mean they have a fear of numbers. They know that intuitively enhanced decision making doesn't preclude rational or logical analysis. They use both—and consider each valid and powerful.

Performance as result of a good system, not a good system as result of better performance.

A new leadership needs to get out from their cultural and expertise silos.

Ability to lead to the unknown

In this persistent and transformative business scenario, leadership today must be able to lead their team/s to the unknown. But what does this mean?

The **exponential technology** innovation we are facing, led by the speed of how the market change is reshaping not only **dynamics, frictions** and **opportunities,** but as well how our audience makes choices, prioritizes, defines their needs and shapes their **behavioral economics.**

So far companies have always had:

- To keep searching for an answer in the known.

- To keep searching for an answer by copying someone or something else.

- To keep searching for an answer by cutting costs.

This is because every idea and tactic always requires a proof of validity from the client side, but future actions based on past information are not always effective.

Instead, we should start searching for answers from a humanity perspective by being inclusive of perspectives regarding the problem's solution; having a holistic view of possible factors playing a role; possessing an organic tactic to take actions in the whole system; and focusing on balancing the value of the entire solution experience.

This is the reason why many new **ways of thinking** (such as Design Thinking), **behavioral sciences** (such as Cognitive analysis) and **data technologies** (such as deep-learning & AI) are rising.

Be focused on creating the conditions to support the team instead of the outcome

For one moment, let's forget process relevance, best practices and making more efficiency.

Be focused on creating the system conditions to support your team instead of the outcome.

This is the key to success for every organization to create incremental competitive advantage, to facilitate innovation and exponential growth. Normally in the world of agencies (but not exclusively) this approach is not always applicable as it does not produce immediate benefits or results, but there are many examples and realities in terms of business and brands where the benefit of this approach has created companies with a growth exponential.

We need a new mental model: serving all constituents well.

- **Alibaba**: Alibaba's chairman and chief executive officer declared that the company's mission was to "make it easy to do business anywhere" and the primary objective has been to build the ecosystem able to make this happen, instead of developing tactics to grow.

- **Xioami**: Xiaomi quickly rose to become one of China's top smartphone manufacturers after its founding in 2010. By mid-2015, it was looking to bolster its declining repeat purchase rate and deepen the impact of its products. The company begins to invest heavily in an "Ecosystem" of allied companies and compatible smart products.

- **Starbucks**: has invested heavily to distribute value all over their business system, from farmers, to employers, to the stores, to the products and ultimately to the community around the stores. Their performance becomes the results of all of them.

- **Apple**: is proof that everything matters in making a product valuable, from the environment where the products are created, to the sustainability and integration in the context, to the sale environment. Remember, Steve Jobs in the '90s fought with the Apple board to transform the aesthetic of the factory because he believed that impacted the experience of the employers and ultimately the results they would produce.

- **David Binder:** "Don't try to find ideas, ideas choose you." David believed, if you are in a good and right environment, good ideas will always show up to you.
(David Binder is a Tony Award-winning Broadway, off-Broadway, and West End theater producer, who has been named the next artistic director of the Brooklyn Academy of Music.)

More Insights
(Search the following sentence in Google to retrieve the link)

- Deloitte - Business ecosystems come to the age

- HRB - How B2B companies can grow with ecosystem orchestration

Never delegate understanding

This mistake happens a lot. When we buy tools and expect them to fix our problems, we're delegating understanding. When we design a strategy and expect others to implement it, we're delegating understanding. When we ignore experiments, iteration and learning and just expect our first ideas to work, we're delegating understanding.

When we try to design better organizations and better outcomes for people, there are no shortcuts. We have to start with building a deep understanding of how they are now and operate within that framework. We can't delegate this work – we have to dig in and do it ourselves.

In 1940, the **Museum of Modern Art of New York** wanted to encourage the design of furniture that enhanced the quality of life for people, regardless of wealth or class. They initiated a design contest called **"Organic Design in Home Furnishings**," defined as: "A design can be called organic if, within the object as a whole, there is a harmonious relationship between the individual elements as regards structure, material, and purpose."

Charles Eames and **Eero Saarinen** won[1] the contest with this chair, working through 3000 studies of the components of ergonomic problems, twice. Ironically, despite the goals of the contest, the Eames/Saarinen chair couldn't be successfully manufactured at the time – it was too complex and too expensive.

Eames found success designing with his wife Ray. They took the failure of the organic chair and delved even more deeply into the problems of design and manufacturing. After thousands more experiments and prototypes, they came out with the DCW Chair – which Time Magazine named the Best Design of the 20th Century.

Never delegate understanding. In this way you can learn how to help other people to understand (to take apart and put back together).

[1] AVERAGE PERFORMANCES AND INNOVATION POWER OF TEAMS WITH DIFFERENT SHARING APTITUDES

A3501 Chair, Organic Design in Home Furnishings winner. (Left)

DCW Chair, Time Magazine named the Best Design of the 20th Century. (right)

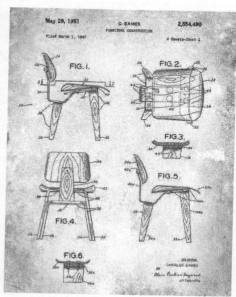

Balance learning and unlearning cultures

It's an understatement to say that we live in a changing world. In fact, the change around is so rapid that experts believe that a major part of what students are learning today will be obsolete a decade later, when they will be working in jobs that are yet to be created.

The corporate world is experiencing revolutions and disruptions at an alarming rate and the "gig economy," the "skill economy" and all the other new economies that make up the modern work world demand a different kind of learning. From the learner's perspective, there is so much to assimilate at any given moment. They don't seem to have much choice, then, but to learn continuously. In this busy time when there is so much learning, now is also the best time to take a pause and consider unlearning, too.

Often, employees are bombarded with so much knowledge through their working hours (and even afterward) that they tend to develop fatigue, and they may have a hard time being receptive to more learning. Unlearning can pave the way for relearning over a period of time. Build a culture of unlearning. Culture is the framework on which the success of an organization's learning (and unlearning) is built. Executive buy-in into the culture is a must.

Unlearning is not a day-long or overnight process, because both learning and unlearning happen through our lifetime. Letting go of what we know and giving way to new ideas demands persistence. Learning new skills is a great way to keep up with market developments, but the process of unlearning empowers us to adapt to change. Learning new skills is a great way to keep up with the market, but the process of unlearning empowers us to adapt to change and reduce friction.

Are you the next Chief Unlearning Officer?

Experience stage: forms of values

The road to failed customer-experience programs is paved with good intentions. Executives are quick to see the end-game benefits of a customer-centric strategy: more satisfied customers, increased loyalty, a lower cost to serve, and more engaged employees. But they often fail to understand clearly what superior customer experience is worth and exactly how it will generate value.

At a recent roundtable, fewer than half of the customer-experience leaders present could say what ten points of net promoter score would be worth to their businesses. E

xecutives launch disruptive initiatives to delight customers with bold moves and innovations. But they often fail to quantify the economic outcomes of differences in customer experiences, so their efforts end up having clear costs and unclear near-term results. Customer-experience transformations invariably raise questions about business policies, cross-functional priorities, and how to invest in innovation.

But they often fail to quantify the economic outcomes of differences in customer experiences, so their efforts end up having clear costs and unclear near-term results. Customer-experience transformations invariably raise questions about business policies, cross-functional priorities, and how to invest in innovation.

Identifying this link between experience and the value provided is never easy, and a lot of factors play a role. However, often we are blind to or see only one of the faces of the experience value.

We can define two sides of the experience value:

- **Value in the experience:** This is the value released during the experience itself, while the audience enjoys it and participates. Almost

90% of an organization is focused on this side trying to create the richest and most integrated experience possible.

- **Value from the experience:** This form of value is what the experience journey leaves in the context of the audience system (or life). Often the result of this value is bigger and more positive (or negative) compared to the other one, rebalancing the entire result. Remember, your audience gets a compulsive result of the experience.

Looking for growth, trust & serendipity

When I think of transparency, my first thought is about sharing what I am really thinking. In order to be fully transparent, you must have massive courage to voice your ideas and opinions so that they are discussed openly. This allows your ideas to be debated freely.

"Radical transparency" is creating a culture that is direct and honest in communication and sharing of company strategies so that all people are trusting and loyal to the continuous evolution of the organization.

For leaders, radical transparency is a way to build trust with their employees. Transparency can create deeper relationships. However, it can also cause resentment within the culture.

When you set out to have transparency, some people will not be able to handle that level of honesty. People begin to internalize the feedback, limiting their ability to be productive.

Ray Dalio, author of the book *Principles* say:

"I want independent thinkers who are going to disagree. The most important things I want are meaningful work and meaningful relationships. And I believe that the way to get those is through radical truth and radical transparency. In order to be successful, we have to have independent thinkers -- so independent that they'll bet against the consensus. You have to put your honest thoughts on the table."

–

Practice being honest and sharing with others how they can improve at every opportunity. As the culture sees the benefit of this, it is going to be easier.

You must make a conscious effort to reduce secrets and having closed-door conversations. Continuous growth requires deeper conversations and when I see leaders embrace radical transparency it can unleash new energy into the culture.

These are all characteristics extremely important in multidisciplinary work environments facing system challenges..

Takeaways

A creative life begins when someone teaches you how to see—not merely look.

–

Inspiring people is key, but understanding how to make things work together and help people to figure out how to change or do their work better, are three factors that cannot be separated.

–

Empower people.

–

Hire people smarter than you.

Business and operative narratives

–

Language defines your thinking and a country's economy.

The role of narratives in business

For a long time, the idea that language might shape thought was considered at best untestable, and more often, simply wrong. Research at Stanford University and at MIT has helped reopen this question. They have collected data from around the world: China, Greece, Chile, Indonesia, Russia, and Aboriginal Australia. **What we have learned is that people who speak different languages do indeed think differently** and that even flukes of grammar can profoundly affect how we see the world.

In English we can say things like, "I broke my arm." Now, in many languages, you couldn't use that construction unless you are a lunatic and you went out looking to break your arm — (LOL 😄) and you succeeded. If it was an accident, you would use a different construction.

You take an event like this, an accident. In English, it's fine to say, "He broke the vase." In a language like Spanish, you might be more likely to say, "The vase broke," or "The vase broke itself." If it's an accident, you wouldn't say that someone did it.

Now, I've given you a couple of examples of how language can profoundly shape the way we think, and how it does so in a variety of ways. Language can have significant effects and even greater consequences. As a result, people who speak different languages will pay attention to different things, depending on what their language usually requires them to do.

In the same way, different business or operative narratives change and shape the way you work, the way you do business and the way you play your role alongside others.

As well, it defines assumptions and expectations.

Defining a proper **Business narrative** to properly explain how your business can help your customers is important, but the **Operative**

narrative is equally important, ie. the narrative that explains who forms your organization (or agency in this case), what to do, how to work together, what role each talent has in pursuing the final result and what this result should be.

The **Operative narrative** defines the operative protocol, the assumptions and expectations of each talent, creating **cohesion, resilience, scalability, inclusion and defines the thought with which to make choices and prioritize.**

More Insights
(Search the following sentence in Google to retrieve the link)

• **Scientific American – Does language shape what we think?**

• **Virgin – How language shapes the way we work.**

• **Fast Company – How language shapes our perception of reality.**

• **PLOS - Future tense and economic decisions: controlling for cultural evolution**

Business narratives

Narratives can be considered true interfaces to establish business dialogues. But what is the use of an interface? An interface is all about creating shared boundaries across two or more separate components, with different goals, languages and assumptions. The use of narratives in business helps us to understand how and why businesses succeed or fail, how they work and how to make them better or grow. A proper business narrative helps the client understand how the agency can support the brand through the lens of the experience system by defining:

- **Assumptions & expectations:** from what the client expects and thinks the agency will do to what the agency thinks and assumes it can do.

- **Area of competence:** the layer of the experience and of the brand platform's system in which agencies should have a voice.

- **Goals:** define the final outcome and the way to measure results.

- **Relationship:** define the type of relationship you want with the client (consultative, executive, pro-active, etc.) and who should be part of these conversations (CMO, CIO, CGO, CEO, Product leaders, etc.)

Due to the variety and nature of each agency, an inappropriate business narrative often becomes the cause of major frictions in the relationship with clients and in achieving goals for both. Over time, a business narrative can change to adapt to new market challenges and reframe a new way of storytelling to help the brand experience system.

More Insights
(Search the following sentence in Google to retrieve the link)

- **HBR – How to build a strategic narrative**

Operational narratives

Often, the internal organization of the agency revolves around the same business narratives of the practices, without properly creating its own narrative appropriate to the structure and its mission.

In particular, this problem appears more strongly in highly multidisciplinary contexts where the operational narrative must be able to give a clear and simple indication of what role every single resource and talent covers, not only in terms of outcome and skillset, but also in terms of final problem solving.

From a system perspective, the internal operational narratives are reduced to:

- **Consulting:** to educate, evaluate and reframe challenges and how to deal with them.

- **Design:** to systemize, connect, transform and simplify.

- **Strategy:** to observe, list and identify gaps & opportunities to grow using tactics.

- **Creativity:** to tell meaningful stories, inspire, change the way of thinking and engage.

- **Delivery:** to build, coordinate and activate.

These forms of narratives often translate, as we will see in subsequent chapters, in groups or departments, sharing the same mindset, goals, assumptions, processes and problems, regardless of team type and outcome.

Transformative narratives

Digital transformation doesn't exist anymore. This term was a real topic in the beginning of 2000 when physical services & businesses started replicating in the digital space, but today the only transformative process related to agencies in the experience economy (or age of systems) are about:

- **Brand transformation:** how do you reshape, transform and fix brand positioning and expectations in a context where how you do things becomes more relevant than what you say or do? How do you define, not a brand mission but a brand thinking, able to be inoculated into the entire ecosystem and integrated with others, in a world where everything matters to make a brand matter? Consistency, systematizing, connecting, simplifying, these are only some of these challenges.

- **Marketing transformation:** how do you transform the way a brand marketing strategy and ecosystem work? How do you engage audiences through systems and benefit from social media, emerging technology and audience influencers to deploy values to your audience? And how should your organization change its way of working or thinking about growing its business in these new audience scenarios? Participation instead of attraction

- **Experience transformation:** how do you create consistency and value in your brand experience, demolish barriers and distinguish between what are products, services or store experiences? How do you create cohesion and integration? Become useful to your audience.

All these transformative narratives play a big role in the Model and Lead layer of each brand system and requires a solid, broad and deep relationship with all the C-suite of the agencies' clients.

Beneficials narratives

Another form of narrative business can be identified in the type of benefit or business goal it hopes to help achieve. Every narrative user works on all the layers of the experience system in an equal way:

- **Consulting**: When agencies support brands with multidisciplinary skills to evaluate every single choice through research, simulations, impact assessments, identification of opportunities, trends and possible issues affecting the growth of the brand.

- **Growth**: This approach is also concerned with all the layers of the system, but focused on identifying gaps, removing frictions, and growing the system as it is organized, without transformations or ambitions of innovation.

- **Innovation**: Focused on all levels, it is dedicated to identifying opportunities for simplification, the integration of emerging technologies and the transformation of the system, creating the conditions not only to scale faster and faster, but also taking the context to stimulate an organic and competitive innovation.
  Often processes of innovation do not produce a growth of the brand or of the explicit business, but they allow growth strategies to do so.

In the ambitions of the agencies in one or more of these offerings and business narratives, it is important to have a clear relationship in the space of necessary skills, assumptions and the type of relationship needed with their clients.

BRAND (AS AN EXPERIENCE), SYSTEM & NARRATIVES MATRIX
Last update January 2019

From a business scenario perspective | From an internal perspective

	BUSINESS NARRATIVES*	TRANSFORMATIVE	BENEFICIAL	OPERATIVE NARRATIVES	
Feed systems	Your narrative				
Lead systems	Your narrative				
Model systems	Your narrative				
				Consulting	Reframe Systems
				Design	Transform Systems
				Strategy	Grow Systems
				Creative	Engage Systems
				Delivery	Activate Systems

* **Business narrative examples:** Branding, Experience, Communication, Advertising, Marketing Automation, CRM etc. Although each agency could argue that it has many more than three skills and therefore business narratives, each layer of the system can be guided by a narrative, including many other capabilities.

Takeaways

Shape your narrative through a system perspective.

–

Narratives change with the audience. Your business narrative will evolve with the market.

–

Similar things can be described in different ways, but that way defines how you deal with these things.

–

Keep aligning your business and operational narratives. Misalignment can cause a negative financial impact.

Team shaping

–

We live in a world where, in the business context, there are no longer distinctions between physical or digital spaces. We live in a world of interconnected systems, in a society of consciousness.

Accidental & intentional teams

In the world of agencies, in the last 20 years we have seen an increase in the diversification of the types of projects, the necessary skills and the technologies used to collaborate, as well as the complexity of the projects themselves.

Sitting at the table of ideas, we have seen not just creatives but strategists, data analysts, experience designers, technologists and often many others, creating not only difficulties in coordinating the project, but increasingly in aligning different mindsets, values and behaviors.

What's more, the growing popularity of agile methodologies has often created the illusion that teams would become agile by assigning the necessary skills when needed, orchestrating everything with a project management method, aligning everyone on sprint design, goals, milestones and feedback.

All this, without taking into account how more and more we bring together not only different skillsets, but also different mindsets with different values and behaviors, thus transforming the Intentional team into an Accidental team.

The cost of having Accidental teams:

1. Individual resources spend more time defending their perspectives within the team than adding value to the project.

2. Lack of collaboration and alignment impacts the quality of results and management costs, without considering the impact it can have on the customer.

3. The frustration and lack of sharing does not allow the formation of culture within the team, its efficiency and consequently the professional growth of each talent.

The advantage of having Intentional teams:

1. Every single resource shares the same objectives and goals, always finding a way, as a group of people (with different abilities and experiences) of agreeing together on group choices.

2. The alignment on how to achieve and evaluate the results not only allows greater cohesion and quality of results, but creates the conditions for greater inclusion of each individual talent regardless of their skillset and experience.

3. The sharing of values and behaviors allows the formation of a culture within the team to allow greater efficiency, professional growth, propensity to scalability and reduction of management costs.

Intentional teams: differences

How they are different:

- **Different mindsets:** Each team has its own mindset, made of assumptions, cultures, goals, behaviors and values.

- **Different methodologies:** Each team develops its own methodology, improves it and transforms it in order to make it replicable, scalable and measurable

- **Different narratives:** Each team facing the system from different perspectives looks for unique and specific values of the goals, and develops its own specific narrative both internal (micro-narrative) and external (narrative business) towards customers.

- **Different outcomes:** Although different intentional teams can share the same skillsets, the different mindset applied leads to different types of outcomes that are specific to each team.

- **Different client relationships:** The type of relationship with the client is also specific to the type of intentional team developed. (ex: co-participatory, collaborative, advisory, executive, etc.)

- **Different accountability:** Following the types of relationships, methodologies and outcomes, each team requires a complete and different form of accountability (ex: by project value, time allocation by budget, by advisory, etc.)

Intentional teams: commonalities

What they share with each other:

- **Skillsets & talent:** Regardless of the type of final outcome, each intentional team can share the same types of talent and skillsets. (ex: a visual designer can sit either in a Creative team, a Design team or in a Strategic team using his/her skills for different outcomes and purposes).

- **Inclusive and multidisciplinary:** Each team becomes inclusive in order to participate and collaborate in the search for the solution of the challenge, and at the same multidisciplinary in maintaining and cultivating the diversity of skills of each participating talent.

- **Scalable & flexible structure:** Each team can scale and adapt according to the amount of work and the type and characteristics of each new talent introduced, allowing professional growth.

- **Knowledge transfer enabled:** Both types of teams manage to transfer their culture and knowledge, thus successfully replicating team models with efficiency.

- **Measurable:** By sharing the same operational model, each team becomes increasingly measurable in terms of performance, efficiency, leaving intact their specific individuality in terms of accountability and type of outcome.

- **Perspective:** Each team is different but at the same time aligned with the others under a single operative perspective.

Goals: problem solving vs outcomes

As we have already pointed out, not all agencies operate with the same skills and goals, therefore, without forgetting the factors linked to the size of the structures, each reality will adapt organizational models to their needs and contexts.

Despite this, we can, however, identify a neutral (or common) operating model that's scalable, flexible and replicable to fit all organizations. In all cases, other factors become critical, such as cultural cohesion, methodology, optimization of resources and stimulation of innovation, which often disappears.

In a context of agencies, the previously mentioned operational narratives define the models of intentional teams, as they not only represent the perspective facing the challenges and projects, but determine the type of (unique) mindsets necessary.

Each team, regardless of the type of outcome (which in some cases may be similar), differs from the type of **mindset used**, the **system perspective** and the **problem solving method** used, creating a clear overlap and internal collaboration framework.

Leaders of **expertise, capabilities, skillsets** or **business opportunities** will work as a new team liaison (such as coaches or navigators). [2]

Small teams

In any modern organization, small teams (from two to six people maximum) are more accountable and agile, which allows them to move quickly, adapting to and reorganizing around new needs.

These features allow a series of competitive advantages:

- **Transparency**: small teams cannot hide anything, benefiting from the organization in terms of integration, inclusion, and the quality of the relationship with their customers.

- **Dedicated**: small teams are dedicated and take care of one thing at a time and not three things at the same time. Each one works on one project at a time, allowing better internal planning, speed of validation, coordination and quality of the result.

- **Co-located & Gentrified:** small teams need constant iteration and consequently must be co-located. In the last 20 years, thanks to new technologies and the growth of project team sizes, more and more remote collaboration has become a necessary constant, but without being advantageous and/or preferable.

  Small teams must therefore avoid "remote collaboration," preferring physical or virtually co-located situations by sharing the same tools, eco-system and time zone.

  The advantage of all this, however, becomes the possibility of each individual team to choose their working location by opening the door to an operational gentrification (in office, out of office, etc.)

- **Cross functional:** Creatives, planners, designers, developers, makers; all these people must "be the same people," by understanding the different perspectives, priorities and methods, working together on the same thing at the same time.

  It's the only way that collaboration can work, otherwise everything returns to an inefficient waterfall process.

- **Autonomous & empowered:** Teams can thus work on their own planning cycle, which allows them to explore, learn, interact and determine their own day-by-day tactical choices, without the need for micro-managing these folks. If they make mistakes, they will figure it out at the end of that cycle and they'll course correct.

Operational model: a new form of distributed organization

Organizational systems must function as a living organism, and therefore must have the autonomy to evolve and a democratic access to participatory resources.

Each resource has a role, a shared and recognized contribution from each one, without discrimination of "importance" between those who think and those who perform, thus creating a cohesive and inclusive context. But how can this self-balancing model manifest itself?

Requirements:

1. Each resource provides a mindset and a specific approach to solving the problem.

2. Each resource provides a skillset and the ability to achieve specific outcomes.

What not to do:

1. Organize teams based on expertise or per account (ex: brand, loyalty, campaigns, etc.). Despite the theoretical cohesion and multidisciplinary nature of these teams, the repetition of the type of work leads to a high specialization but also to a creative and professional stagnation, preventing the creation of the conditions to innovate and often causing high turnover of talent.

    In addition, teams based on expertise create a bubble effect, which in the long run leads to a clear problem of cultural silos. (ex: "We do not work with that team because we do not understand each other.")

2. Organize teams based on capabilities: (ex: Engagement strategy, Art, UX, etc.). In the long term, this organizational model does not facilitate cohesion and integrated multidisciplinary, and often creates frictions between groups due to different operational narratives and mindsets.

Therefore, the main problem of this organizational model is the occurrence of those so-called "accidental teams" mentioned above, where each resource is working with different talent from project to project, with different methods, assumptions and goals.

What to do:

What is needed is to create a highly resilient, serendipitous, replicable, measurable, scalable, efficient, decentralized and cohesive structure.

1. Organize **micro-teams by operational narrative** (or mindset), where the type of group outcome is determined by the type of talent included and the type of capabilities they bring with them.
    The same capabilities (ex: visual designers, engagement strategists, etc.) can be present in different micro-teams, in different intentional groups. [1]

2. **Lead, but leave each micro-team to self-manage**, to allocate resources, to plan and to define methodologies and tactics. The team will then identify a coordinating leader from within the group. [1-A/B]

3. Allocate **each project or task to the team and not to the individual resource**. Then the team decides whether 33% of three resources or 100% of a resource is required to resolve the request. [1-A/B]

4. **Identify expertise leaders across groups and teams** capable of guiding and developing new forms of specific narratives, tactics and cultural and strategic cohesion. (ex: Lead Customer Experience Strategist; Lead Visual Designer.) [2]

5. **Identify intentional groups leaders,** dedicated to coordinating and making the organization and the day-to-day needs of their group and integration with the other groups as efficient as possible. [2]

There are also many necessary interfacing activities with customers, as each group must have direct access to the consultative dialogue with the customers, but every single agency must adapt a specific solution to its offering. [3]

[1-A] INTENTIONAL TEAM GROUPS,CAPABILITIES AND CHARACTERISTICS
Ideal organization of an Intentional team in a large agency.

Operational Narrative	Behavioral goals group	Time frame goals	Intentional Teams
Consulting	Educate, Evaluate and Re-frame.	Long-term	Team 1, team 2, teamN..
Design	Systemize, Transform and Simplify.	Medium-long term	**Team 1, team 2, teamN..**
Strategy	Run, Listen and Grow.	Medium-term	Team 1, team 2, teamN..
Creative	Tell Stories, Inspire and Engage.	short-medium term	Team 1, team 2, teamN..
Delivery	Produce, Coordinate and Activate	short term	Team 1, team 2, teamN..

Capabilities Capabilities Capabilities Capabilities Capabilities Capabilities Capabilities Capabilities Capabilities Capabilities Capabilities Capabilities Capabilities Capabilities

Traditional capabilities of the agencies are the results of
the cross-disciplinal and mindset works of multiple team.

139

[1-B] INTENTIONAL TEAM FINGERPRINTS
Ideal organization of an Intentional team in a large agency.

Team fingerprint

Team 1

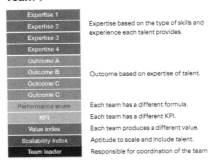

Expertise 1	Expertise based on the type of skills and experience each talent provides.
Expertise 2	
Expertise 3	
Expertise 4	
Outcome A	
Outcome B	Outcome based on expertise of talent.
Outcome C	
Outcome C	
Performance score	Each team has a different formula.
KPI	Each team has a different KPI.
Value index	Each team produces a different value.
Scalability index	Aptitude to scale and include talent.
Team leader	Responsible for coordination of the team

[2] INTENTIONAL TEAM BY OUTCOME & EXPERTISE
Ideal organization of an Intentional team in a large agency.

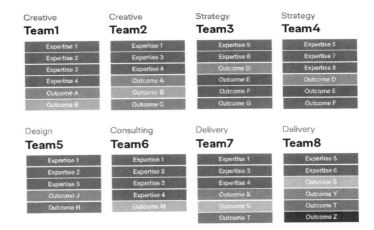

LEADERS TYPE

Capabilities leaders: Leader across team groups
Mindset group leaders: Leader across teams
Team leaders: Team member's leaders

[3] IDEAL ORGANIZATION OF AN INTENTIONAL TEAM IN MEDIUM OR SMALL ORGANIZATION (EXAMPLE)

Traditional advertising agencies

Consulting	Educate, Evaluate and Re-frame.
Design	Systemize, Transform and Simplify.
Strategy	Run, Listen and Grow.
Creative	Tell Stories, Inspire and Engage.
Delivery	Produce, Coordinate and Activate.

Traditional experience agencies

Consulting	Educate, Evaluate and Re-frame.
Design	Systemize, Transform and Simplify.
Strategy	Run, Listen and Grow.
Creative	Tell Stories, Inspire and Engage.
Delivery	Produce, Coordinate and Activate.

Traditional marketing agencies

Consulting	Educate, Evaluate and Re-frame.
Design	Systemize, Transform and Simplify.
Strategy	Run, Listen and Grow.
Creative	Tell Stories, Inspire and Engage.
Delivery	Produce, Coordinate and Activate.

Traditional digital agencies

Consulting	Educate, Evaluate and Re-frame.
Design	Systemize, Transform and Simplify.
Strategy	Run, Listen and Grow.
Creative	Tell Stories, Inspire and Engage.
Delivery	Produce, Coordinate and Activate.

Behavioral superpowers

Your superpower is the role that you are put on this Earth to contribute. It's what you do better than anyone else on the team. Tapping into it more often will not only help your team, but you'll find your work more satisfying, too.

Why is it important to be aware of the talents and behavioral superpowers of the team?

Because these hidden skills are what could make a team successful, boost efficiency, create cohesion, inclusion, and create the conditions to trigger innovation.

Each superpower plays a key role in solving complex and systematic problems, especially in different mindsets.

A team focused on **growing and leading** a system (by strategy) must have a great aptitude for **identifying opportunities** (gap detections), **deconstructing complex situation** (complexity burst), **understanding people and clients** (empathy and cultural compass) and be **able to make choices** under pressure and unstuck situations (decisiveness).

Without these characteristics, a team will probably consume more time, more effort, and more resources to achieve their goals, creating frustrations amongst talent and frictions with clients.

It's so important to be aware of your team's and talent's superpowers, as well as their skillsets and mindsets to develop a proper creative and innovative team culture, aside from all the competitive and economical benefits.

What's your superpower?

BEHAVIORAL SUPERPOWERS MAPPING

Mapping provided by S/Y Partners – For more informations superpowers.sypartners.com

Motivation	Empathy	Vision	Recalibration	Grit
Negotiation	Evangelizing	Cultural Compass	Pattern Mapping	System Thinking
Decisiveness	Complexity Busting	Peacemaking	Experimentation	Provocation
Gap Detection	Harmonizing	Ingenuity	Problem Solving	Creative Thinking

Behavioral superpower characteristics:

- **Motivation**: They have many tricks in their bag—some loving, some tough—and they know exactly what will work for whom. They can help people remember why the work matters and reinforce how each person's contribution makes a difference.

- **Empathy**: With antennae up, they pick up on the needs and emotions around them, even when someone isn't saying anything. They are great stand-ins when the team is trying to build a relationship with someone and needs to find the right way in.

- **Vision**: They can see a future destination in vivid color. Along with providing an initial push, visionaries can help the team keep its ambition high throughout the journey.

- **Recalibration**: They are the eye in the center of the storm—clear, focused, in control, and unfazed by the disruptions around them. They can soothe and reassure teammates, and help the team get back on track.

- **Grit**: They are the quiet engine of the team—able to keep pushing themselves and the work until it is truly done. They can motivate teammates to keep going too, especially when the work is more of a marathon than a sprint.

- **Negotiation**: They can quickly build bonds but never let those relationships cloud their judgment. Negotiators can be invaluable to the team whenever they need to broker a deal.

- **Evangelizing**: They don't try to sell anyone on anything. They simply tell great stories about what they love...and the next thing you know, people are lining up to have some of what they're having. Evangelizers are great to bring in when the team needs to translate its work to a wider audience—especially an audience that may be skeptical.

- **Cultural Compass:** He or she knows when the team is going against its character. And when the team seriously starts to lose its way, the cultural compass will gently but firmly ask questions until a new course is set.

- **Pattern Mapping:** They are always in a mode of inquiry—asking questions, mapping similarities, chasing after the logic. They can help the team find shortcuts at the start of a new endeavor.

- **System Thinking:** They travel to the outer edges of a problem, then work their way back to reveal all the parts and how they connect. They can help a team think through the pros and cons of various options.

- **Decisiveness:** With confidence and speed, they break down the choices, weigh each one, and make the call. Deciders opt for pragmatism over perfectionism, because they know there's no ideal answer. They can help the team summon the bravery to make a choice—and feel OK about it afterward.

- **Complexity busting:** They cut through layers of information to find the most important ideas. They're great to tap when the team has a huge amount of research but isn't sure what it all means.

- **Peacemaking:** They have the ability to convey loyalty to everyone while never taking sides. When the team is at odds and work is threatening to grind to a halt, a peacemaker can get the team back on track.

- **Experimentation:** They're able to rapidly generate many ideas, zero in on the most promising ones, put them into motion, and refine along the way.

Experimenters can help when the team is experiencing "analysis paralysis" and can't take action—or when it simply can't come up with enough new ideas.

- **Provocation:** They are much more concerned with being effective than with being liked. The team needs them most when the work lacks originality or everyone is playing it too safe.

- **Gap detection:** They easily ferret out mistakes, sloppy thinking, logical disconnects, short-sightedness in planning, and a host of other problems a team may have but not see. While their talent sometimes goes unappreciated, the best Gap Detectors can be invaluable to a team—finding holes before the team falls in them.

- **Harmonizing:** With equal skill in communication and organization, Harmonizers will try to make sense of everyone on the team, then find a way to play to each person's strengths. With a Harmonizer on board, the team finds its rhythm.

- **Ingenuity:** They mix whatever resources they have on hand with a helping of imagination and a dose of can-do optimism. They are amazing collaborators at the eleventh hour, when time is running out and the stakes are high, or when budgets and staffing have taken a hit.

- **Problem solving:** Like an urgent-care doctor doing an intake, they'll ask just enough questions to assess what's going wrong and why. Problem Solvers can be of great help to a team that has hit a dead end and feels stuck.

- **Creative thinking:** They're the people the team relies on to solve problems in clever, original ways. That's because they can see what's not yet real, and then make it real.

Superpowers definitions by SYPartners – For more informations superpowers.sypartners.com

FREQUENT DISTRIBUTIONS OF BEHAVIORAL SUPERPOWERS THROUGH MINDSET

CONSULTING

DESIGN

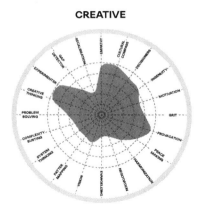

STRATEGY

CREATIVE

DELIVERY

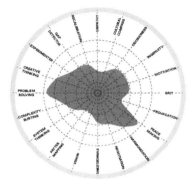

Takeaways

Everyone must have a role in the big picture.

–

Share a unique perspective of a cohesive way of thinking.

–

Create teams by design.

Team & skills inclusion

–

Inclusion is not bringing people into what already exists; it is making a new space, a better space for everyone.

Skillset and problem solving approach

Each talent should not be identified only by the type of skillset and outcome value they can bring within the organization, but also by a number of other factors that go beyond social, behavioral or superpower aspects. In particular, I refer to the personal capacity to **deconstruct** and **face solutions** to problems and/or daily challenges.

Placing a team or several teams on a problem solving dimension effectively eliminates any hierarchical form, creating greater participation and inclusion where each individual can contribute equally to the other members in achieving the goal. Often in the world of agencies this aspect is always secondary, as it is considered an additional contribution by each individual member who is not in a position of leadership.

This declassification is often caused by the fact that different problem solving skills are linked to different approaches, methods and processes, often not immediately understood by other members as a result of assumptions and experiences accumulated through business cases. In part, this problem is solved through the organization of "**problem solving intentional teams**" with **system perspectives** as we have previously seen. It is also true that often there is no shared awareness of this competency except for the perception of some managers toward the talent they manage.

More Insights
(Search the following sentence in Google to retrieve the link)

- **HBR - The two traits of the best problem-solving teams**

- **HBR - A Dedicated team of problem solvers can help big companies act like lean startups**

Establish a shared knowledge transfer system

In ancient times, great civilizations have always developed around trade, agriculture, but especially around the ability to transfer knowledge from individual to individual so the whole society could benefit from it.

It is clear the value that the ability to share knowledge can give to every organization in terms of efficiency, growth, innovation and competitiveness, but very often establishing a **"knowledge transfer system,"** is **erroneously never a priority of leadership or the C-suite.**

Yet a shared system of knowledge transfer allows a more rapid decision-making capacity due to the sharing of problem-solving experiences and their systematization.

It also reduces the loss of know-how, enriching narrative businesses, improving delivery to customers/clients and stimulating innovation and growth.

How do you do this? There are no methods that work for everyone, so each reality will have to establish its own.

But there are little things you can do to establish this knowledge transfer system protocol:

1. **Initiate moments** of multidisciplinary conversation tables periodically.

2. **Create spaces** in your office to support these constant conversations.

3. **Share**. Even a single email is sufficient to align an entire team of an opportunity, a condition or a theme, fueling the narratives of the organization.

More Insights
(Search the following sentence in Google to retrieve the link)

- **HBR - Seven factors of great office design**

- **Brookings - How office design can catalyze an innovative culture**

- **Forbes - Six key steps to influencing effective knowledge transfer in your business**

Democratized conversation with unstuck protocols

Democratic access to conversation with every internal resource is crucial not only in building transparency, but also confidence.

Ray Dalio, an American billionaire investor, hedge fund manager, and philanthropist, in his book *Principles* explains how trust & transparency are the basic conditions for creating and running a business, and how these are the result of good dialogue.

However, the freedom of access to people and the democratization of conversations, in large realities, often turns into a management problem where questions and problems are often brought to the table of people not competent, or often generating misunderstandings, frustrations, confusion and static.

Here, the lack of a clear definition not only of roles, but also responsibilities becomes key.

Very often once again, the leadership forgets how properly balancing access to conversation with a simple form of structure and responsibility becomes necessary.

For example, within projects with more teams involved and where inclusiveness offers a democratic conversation amongst talent, the team needs to be guided by a protocol that defines what choices to make to unlock situations (ex: operational narrative/mindset) of deadlock autonomously.

Keith Yamashita, founder and chairman of **SYPartners** has developed an entire culture around unstuck teams and an organization's leaders in the complex decision making process.

More Insights
(Search the following sentence in Google to retrieve the link)

- **HBR - Getting teams unstuck**

- **iTunes Books - Principles, Ray Dailo**

- **Amazon - Unstuck: A tool for yourself, your team, and your world**

Create multiple career paths

As you know, everyone's professional life is never straightforward because of external or contextual factors that are not dependent on us, and because we too, like every living form, evolve and change. Therefore, the organizational system of an agency needs to consider how different talent can change over time and undertake related but different careers path.

Not all people have the same attitudes: there are those who have a predisposition to the management of groups and those who do not. There are those who love the relationship with customers and those who do not.

There are those who are the best at building the structure, but prefer to continue crafting the outcome. Consolidating or innovating, managing or creating, these are all individual choices..

Each agency should identify options for progression, supporting personal and natural personalities:

1. **Competence**: we grow in competence and seniority, becoming an individual (or leader) capable of developing and guiding the culture of our cross-team expertise in the entire organization without managerial or client-facing responsibilities. (ex: Lead CX Strategist)

2. **Organizational**: we grow in the experience of orchestrating the best talent in our area of expertise (and similar*), focusing on the efficiency, outcome of the outcome and in the creation of the innovative and growth conditions. (ex: Director CX Strategy)

3. **Business**: we grow and evolve with the aim of developing new forms of business and opportunities in the face of the market and customers, enriching the narrative business and defining the direction/vision of the agency in relation to a specific (and similar*) competency. (ex: Principal CX Strategy)

Talents, in their maturing and evolving can change or embrace more skills. (ex: Designer to strategy)

Takeaways

Different thinker must be protected and supported. Organization system have an aptitude to soffocate unusual behaviors.

Scalability & resilience

–

**There is a difference between adapting to resist or changing to keep growing.
Only the latter allows you to be a leader.**

Unique KPIs for micro-teams

There are many factors that impact performance, especially in the case of intentional teams. Each team not only must have different metrics depending on the type of problems that are to be solved, but also different forms of assessment depending on the type of outcome, team size and their characteristics.

Why is this important? Because in a multidisciplinary and inclusive organization like this it becomes difficult to compare teams only according to the result.

Two teams can reach the same outcome, but through different paths and processes that in turn bring a different value and/or meaning to the customers.

Other factors to consider in addition to a basic solution/time ratio required are:

- **Knowledge produced:** Knowledge is generated during each project. Knowledge that, if properly shared, will change in the short/medium term into a competitive and time-saving advantage, then as a consequence, into an implicit monetization added to the amount paid by the customer.

- **Innovation generated:** Similar to the knowledge produced, the innovation generated (solving a problem or forging a solution in a different way), becomes not only a competitive advantage if properly shared internally, but also a business case for potential new business and consequently, an implicit monetization.

- **Systemization created:** The optimization of the creative process and of the journey to the solution through a systematization of methods, assets or other, in the short/medium term turns out to be a time-saving advantage and therefore still an implicit monetization.

- **Incubation Rate:** If new talent is being incubated in the team, we should add a positive balancing value to the team KPIs. This is because normally elements of the team have to dedicate a portion of time in the form of training or mentorship to new members thus lowering the performance, but producing added value also considered an implicit monetization.

Incubate and train new talent

Incubating new talent, training them and preparing them to integrate into the company's dynamics, as already mentioned are values produced, but often not included as an index of monetization.

In a context of intentional teams, for each team we can introduce a new member from time to time to prepare and align with the team's methodologies and performance. In this way new members are not only protected and supported by the team, but they are allowed to compare and share with other team members, reducing frustration, confusion and/or loss.

Once enough new members are incubated, the team is ready to be cloned by creating two new distinct teams, sharing the same methods, knowledge and performances.

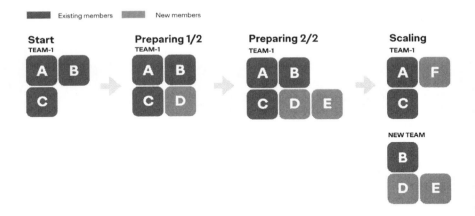

Diversification and transformation tactics

The management of intentional teams, allows a perfect strategy to climb the creative and productive capacity, while maintaining a coherent methodological culture and ensuring an inclusive multidisciplinary team. This creates the conditions for transformations by serendipity and diversification of skills that in the **medium to long term allow a better resilience to market changes.**

Inclusion of new talent in existing teams–talent with different skills and competencies that do not impact the type of value each team must generate–**allows us a greater flexibility in welcoming talent with skills that normally we could not justify** in terms of accountability (resources planned by skills).

This offers us not only the flexibility to invest in strategic competencies that the agencies consider necessary to have in portfolios to stimulate internal transformations, but also gives us the **freedom and flexibility for talent who want to experience new challenges,** to change teams or micro-teams easily.

Micro-teams: a competitive advantage

Jeff Bezos has a rule at **Amazon**, or perhaps more aptly a philosophy. If a team cannot be fed by two pizzas then that team is too large. The reasoning is quite straightforward and basic.

More people means more communication, more bureaucracy, more chaos, and more of pretty much everything that slows things down, hence why large organizations are oftentimes pegged as being so inefficient.

A study was conducted by three professors from **UCLA** (Staats), **Penn State** (Milkman), and **Chapel Hill** (Fox). In the experiments that these professors ran they utilized **LEGO** bricks and two teams comprised of either two people or four people. The goal was to see which team could put together a certain LEGO structure together.

By now you shouldn't be surprised to know that the team comprised of **2 people accomplished the task in 36 minutes** whereas the **team comprised of 4 people finished the task in 56 minutes.**

Organizations should really think about what their team structures look like, and I would encourage them to create and follow similar "two pizza rules."

It's no coincidence that smaller organizations are oftentimes more nimble and agile, while large organizations look like they are walking through sludge.

Last but not least:

- Small teams are more entrepreneurial and they also move faster.

- People in small teams trust each other.

- They don't waste your human resources.

- Small teams foster mentoring.

- Out of necessity, small teams become meritocracies.

Agility & management

In a conversation prepping for an upcoming workshop/event someone said to me, "*Our tech teams are learning **Agile**. Our product teams are learning Lean and our design teams are learning **Design Thinking**. Which one is right?*"

The question of which one is "right" came about because the seemingly competing trainings put the various disciplines on different cadences, with different practices targeting different objectives. The collaboration, shared understanding and increased productivity they were all promised were nowhere to be found.

This is not the first case where I've come across this challenge and it's not surprising. The productization of **Agile** adoption along with increased interest in the **Lean Startup** method in the enterprise and **Design Thinking** has led various coaches and trainers to focus narrowly on one of these ideas and then market their services to the audience they believed was most likely to buy. Well-meaning managers trained their teams within their discipline and never thought to look beyond because their new coaches never suggested it.

The net result? Confusion at best. Chaos at worst.

Teams that were supposed to start building trust through cross-functional collaboration are now at odds about how to start, who does what and what their ultimate goal was. Tech teams were focused on increasing velocity. Product teams were focused on reducing waste. Design teams wanted lengthy, upfront research and design phases to help discover what the teams should work on. Very quickly they found themselves pulling away from each other, as opposed to collaborating more effectively.

This is the reason why organizing teams around the system perspective (the closest to the perspective of the audience) leads to align all the participants in a project with a single shared common perspective. Each intentional team will be able to define its own methodology according to its priority whether it is to increase speed, optimization or learning, allowing other teams to interact and to agree on operational choices, creating a transparent and participatory relationship with the customers themselves.

The alignment of mindsets and methods not only reduces potential incoordination between teams but allows a new and precise measurement of the product value and of the creative process, a factor often highly criticized or misunderstood by the clients of the agencies.

Most popular methodologies used in today business.
* Scrum, Kanban, Crystal, Future Driven Development, Extreme Programming, etc.

Methods	Design thinking	Lean	Agile methods*
Goal	Explore	Learn	Adapt
Focus	Systematizing	Optimization	Efficiency
Approach	Reframe	Listen	Share
Value	Innovation	Knowledge	Time saving
Thinking	Responding to human needs over the solution plan.	Responding to learning over the system plan.	Responding to changes over following the plan.

More Insights
(Search the following sentence in Google to retrieve the link)

• **HBR - Agile at scale**

• **McKinsey - The keys to organizational agility**

Takeaways

Teams are resilient to the context. Do: create the conditions to scale. Don't: focus on scaling a team/s.

Innovation seeking

–

Innovation cannot be an outcome.

Innovation in the experience economy

What is innovation? And what becomes innovation in a context of the experience economy and therefore business? Erroneously, when we think of innovation we always think of technological innovation in the form of new technologies or products and we talk about it as if innovation was a goal or an outcome of an individual, a team or a company.

The reality is that innovation cannot be pursued for itself. All we can do is create the conditions for making the innovation happen, but we'll talk about this in the next chapter.

Airbnb and **UBER** were appointed several times as disruptors in the hospitality and mobility businesses in many cities. But if observed for what they are, software platforms, we discover that the entire technology stack is made of non-proprietary technologies (at least 95%), and that each of us, absurdly, could build a service like Airbnb or Uber in a day, buying the licenses of these well-known technologies from each company owner.

Today, we build complicated and sophisticated solutions without needing to understand how they function and succeed in innovating, instead by focusing on how these **LEGO** bricks (stacks) allow you to make your business work the way you want.

"Innovation" in business today is all about *how you do* things and less about *what you do*. It is more an elegant integration of known elements than of brand new elements.

Changing perspectives, adopting a new way of thinking and creating the right conditions trigger ways to do things differently.

Create the conditions to innovate, not search for innovation

We should understand innovation as an emergent factor of systems.

Executing innovative ideas requires a new way of doing things, often summarized as creativity. And creativity thrives in a work environment that fits the dynamic needs of modern teams, from hyper-collaboration to heads-down time. As today's organizations strive to become more innovative and resilient, they must adapt their spaces and modes of working to promote creative problem-solving across teams.

W. Edwards Deming anticipated this problem in his *Theory of Profound Knowledge* when he said: "the most important figures that one needs for management are unknown and unknowable." The best example of this unknown/unknowable duality is "trust."

Most of us would recognize that trusting environments and relationships are an essential part of a working innovation ecosystem – likely the single most important feature of those systems.

As with gardeners tending the soil, the same is so with leading innovation. It's what you can't see, the soil beneath the surface, that will cause your garden to flourish. **Pay as much attention to the unseen, the unknowable, the unmeasurable, as you do to what's on the surface. Grow in your own confidence to live in the world of uncertainty, trusting your judgment to "know the unknowable." Your innovation garden will be all the better for it.**

How to seek & trigger innovation

Ok, innovation is a result of a good system, but if we wanted to indicate a sort of formula to stimulate innovation, what could it be? If innovation as we have said comes about when we do things differently, then we need new perspectives that allow us to simplify sophisticated solutions or systems.

If we consider a team as elements of a system within a specific context (their experience and the culture of the working space) with a specific purpose (solving the client's challenges), it translates into the classic triad that defines the rule of the interfaces.

Each interface is the result of the relationship between context, elements and function, so to change the interface (and innovate) it is necessary to change one of the factors. So if we are unable to change the function or context, then we can change elements in it.

Some call it "Lateral Thinking" or "Think Different," but in the end both seek the introduction of exotic elements (external and not present in your organization, products or services system) able to influence and change the way in which the elements of the system relate to the context and are associated with delivering the solution.

Common seeking tactics:

- **Lateral thinking:** view the problem from different perspectives.

- **Hacking**: deconstruct and re-build. Permutation & use.

- **Compare patterns:** find similar patterns in different environments & compare them.

More Insights

(Search the following sentence in Google to retrieve the link)

- **HBR - 4 Ways to build an Innovative team**

- **Amazon - The leader's guide to lateral thinking skills – Paul Sloane.**

Reframe briefs, stay focus on the value of the solution

The customer briefs will always be framed by a different perspective used by intentional teams.

It is so important to define a new process to reformulate the client's brief under the lens of the systems and remain focused not just to solve a problem or challenge, but to add value to the system by avoiding the mentioned problem. Without reframing, intentional teams will always work in opposite directions.

Less rules, more serendipity

A decentralized organization, with limited hierarchical structure and democratic access to each resource and asset of the organization, not only simplifies internal bureaucracy and speeds up changes, but also stimulates serendipitous opportunities.

More Insights
(Search the following sentence in Google to retrieve the link)

- **HBR - When success is born out of serendipity**

Empower people

There is a tremendous shift from telling everyone what to do, to empowering others to come up with the best and brightest ideas that have never been thought of before.

This is how you empower people to be their best.

The benefits of this distribution of power are many, from gathering valuable input to having more productive employees; from having a more engaged workforce to helping your company embrace change and make your employees feel more appreciated.

However the dark side of empowering people without a proper knowledge transfer system, cohesive vision and frequent conversation, leads to "cultural bubbles" in the work stage, stagnation and friction caused by misaligned cultural silos.

More Insights
(Search the following sentence in Google to retrieve the link)

- **Empowerment — How to empower people and extend your influence as a leader**

- **Inc - 6 Ways to empower people to be their best**

- **Forbes - 10 Powerful ways to empower your employees**

Share, share & share

People protecting their personal power are being secretive. They believe that if they know more than everyone else, they will remain more important.

Real talent & leaders communicate a lot. They make it a point to share as much information as possible with everybody as it is the only way to validate knowledge, seed changes and discover new things. They see additional power in having a well-informed team that can contribute more because they know more.

Effective talent & leaders win people over by building an open environment of trust and respect. They create meaning for people so they can feel proud of their work. They offer personal recognition. They go out of their way to make the work matter to the people doing it.

An organization accustomed to sharing knowledge as ordinary routine, is more inclined to create serendipitous situations and lead to innovation more frequently (**knowledge transfer system** becomes decisive).

However, a phenomenon was observed during a contest organized by a nonprofit organization called Sage Bionetworks. Analyzing the impact of a knowledge sharing system between teams in terms of performance and innovation, over a long time period, they started to be less competitive and innovative compared to the independent teams.

This very interesting finding suggests that even a highly capable team might miss important insights that other teams, working independently, might capture.

This is why the balance of empowering people and sharing behaviors must always be treated as an indissoluble duo. [1]

[1] AVERAGE PERFORMANCE AND INNOVATIVE POWER OF TEAMS WITH DIFFERENT SHARING APTITUDES.

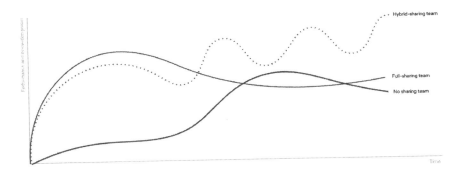

What if errors and mistakes could be monetized?

Unusual in the world of agencies and marketing but ordinary in the world of product development, services and business incubation, is the concept of embracing the failure of an idea, action or a project as a positive and not a negative value, and seeing it as acceptable.

In fact, thoughts such as "design thinking" consider failure or error as an important element to produce "knowledge" and thus become a competitive advantage, if not an opportunity, for a serendipity of dissociated factors.

Integrating this ability to reconsider (reframe) the possible failure or error of an idea as a kind of positive value not only changes the perspective and the degree of risk on the part of customers, but allows agencies to experiment more and more actively.

But how do we properly introduce the concept of "the value-of-failure"? The only way is to have a systematic view of the brand, as an experience, and as part of a larger system (system of systems), reacting as a "living-organism".

With this perspective and approach, we cannot only change the parameters of measurement and evaluation, but also react faster and more effectively by increasing the advisory role that agencies today have lost in some instances, but are actively seeking.

More Insights
(Search the following sentence in Google to retrieve the link)

- **Inc - The value of failure--and danger of success**

- **HBR - The value of failure**

Next step: How can I defeat myself?

A very popular post by **Alberto Brea**, an Executive Director & Consultant, say:

> "**Amazon did not kill the retail industry**, They did it to themselves with a bad customer service."

> "**Netflix did not kill blockbuster**. They did it to themselves with ridiculous late fees."

> "**Uber did not kill the taxi business**. They did it to themselves with limited the number of taxi and the fare control."

> "**Airbnb did not kill the hotel industry**. They did it to themselves with limited availability and pricing options."

Whether you agree or disagree with this concept, what I find extremely insightful in this post is, if brands and businesses are to **survive and remain competitive, innovation must be sought from within the organization and not outside.**

In the search for incremental innovation, every agency and brand, especially when business is good, should ask: **How can I kill the business?** Then, ask participants to place all their ideas up on a whiteboard.

Organize these by smallest-to-largest threat, or by easiest-to-hardest to address. Where are your biggest threat clusters?

Clusters of kill tactics indicate areas that need immediate attention. Once there's consensus on your top three threats, ask everyone for ideas on how they'd prevent these from happening; maybe an acquisition to expand your customer base? Other ideas? This is the moment when goals start being clarified and your issues find solutions..

"How to kill the company" identifies exactly where and how your **business is vulnerable.** It empowers employees, and it helps leaders work on weaknesses while seizing opportunities.

By killing your own company at least once a year, you'll prevent anyone else from writing its actual obituary.

Takeaways

Open conversations able to brake silos and hierarchy.

–

Transparency and vision.

–

Innovation is always where leadership is afraid to go, because that place is not designed yet.

Transformation & adoption

–

A systematic change require a systematic method.

Transformation cannot be imposed, transformation must be inclusive & participative

This is the most important takeaway from this section: Transformational processes cannot be imposed from top to bottom, but must be participatory, inclusive and spread organically throughout the organization.

At the same time, a strong shared vision and guidance from leadership are needed to adopt and support a new company culture and trigger systematic change.

Culture is made up of the unspoken rules that drive behavior, especially behaviors that nobody pays attention to but that are repeated. That repeated behavior is your company's culture.

Many change management tactics move at different process altitudes and transformative dynamics, from the research and definition of a "company culture" to its validation and implementation throughout the structure.

Over time, **McKinsey** developed a clear and measurable method to trigger change management organically, based on four building blocks:

- Role Modeling - *"I see my leaders, colleagues and staff behaving differently."*

- Fostering understanding and conviction - *"I understand what is being asked of me and it makes sense."*

- Developing talent and their skills - *"I have the skills and opportunities to behave in the new way."*

- Reinforcing with formal mechanisms - *"I see that our structures, process, and systems support the changes I am being asked to make."*

This approach starts from the premise of the existence of a company culture in the leadership to use and play as role-model that allows the process to start and ensure that the other building blocks can occur.

When this shared vision and culture in leadership is lacking, it is customary to search within the existing or emerging internal subculture of the company, or in the case of their lack, to prototype new ones.

Leverage subcultures

Subcultures are normally identifiable as isolated teams, which over time, within the company have had the opportunity to develop their own operational culture with clear results of success.

In these cases, the company gives the opportunity to apply and scale the same model to other groups, testing it and measuring its impact.

However, while this method at first sight would seem like the best approach, it suffers in the consideration that often the composition of the team, its characteristics and skills are factors that determine its success, its scalability or bankruptcy.

The same operating model, in a team of different people, may not work.

Prototyped Subcultures

To build the context so that a new corporate subculture can be formed, create a new operative model and team, which can act as a role model.

Often what the company does in these cases, is create a team with a wide diversity of talent and thought, supporting them with proven processes and new working methods, as a guide in the formation of the new model of thought.

This approach, although being the safest way to create a new subculture from within that's measurable, replicable and scalable, tends to produce incremental rather than exponential innovations for reasons of limited diversity and inclusion.

The risk of having to release or retrain resources because they are not compatible with the new subculture remains high, limiting its scalability.

Conclusion

It is indisputable that change should come from within the structure, but it is equally true that innovation only takes place when, exotic factors (external and not present in the organization) enter a new context offering new perspectives and a new way of thinking.

This is why the transformative and identification processes of a new subculture become complex and often require hybrid and continuous approaches.

Management transformation by Design: an organization as a system

Leveraging design as a method to lead a transformation process in the management and leadership of companies is always a more efficient and successful way to achieve an organization's business goals.

Why Design?

Design is often identified as an outcome, but design is a process and mindset for delivering a specific type of outcome.

Design is operating in what is known as the four orders of design:

- **Design for signs & symbols** (almost all types of aesthetic outcomes)

- **Design for things** (devices, furniture, clothing, objects, etc.)

- **Design for actions** (services and processes in digital and physical spaces)

- **Design for systems** (any sort of system-based rules, patterns, organizations etc.)

In all these spaces, the outcome is considered a result of a design process.

Why Design as a way of thinking?

Design from a system perspective is all about systemizing, transforming and simplifying and because organizations are systems of people and operations, you can use it as an operative mindset (protocol) to make choices and actions in the direction of a system solutions.

FOURTH ORDER OF DESIGN

Design Research and the New Learning (2001)
Richard Buchanan, Professor of Design & Management

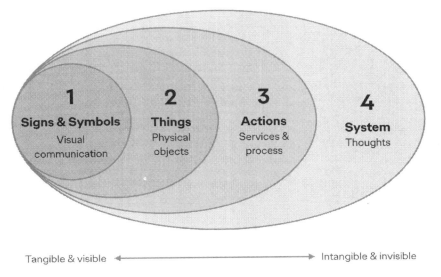

1
Signs & Symbols
Visual
communication

2
Things
Physical
objects

3
Actions
Services &
process

4
System
Thoughts

Tangible & visible ⟵———————————⟶ Intangible & invisible

Design to lead transformation in an uncertain path

When does a way of thinking become valuable?
When we have to make choices in an uncertain path.

Design is a roundtrip journey, often forgotten, with two distinct journeys:

- **A journey to a destination** (seek a vision & frame the problem)
  This process is all about discovering how to add value to the system, along a path made by ideas, prototypes, mistakes, failures, successes, learning, discovery, etc.
  This phase is usually the most used and identified in typical "Design Thinking" workshops. [1]

- **A journey back home** (make the vision happen & solve the problem)
  A process all about how to change the system to lead to the new value, along a path by opening minds, re-framing, re-organizing, educating, etc. This second phase often is identified by "Design Doing." [2]

In an organization (such as a system), the journey back home is known, as well, as an "adoption process," since the company has to adopt a new form of behavior and new elements.

Here is where design becomes helpful in management (as a system) transformation.

[1] A JOURNEY TO A DESTINATION
Seek a vision & frame the problem (Design Thinking)
Multiple hypothesis
Multiple visions

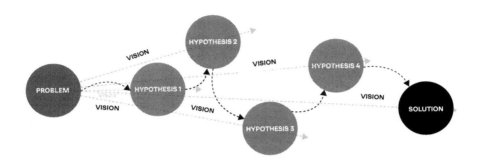

Vision & Assumptions	Reframe a new strategy	Reframe a new strategy	Reframe a new strategy	Reframe a new strategy	Best value of the solution.

[2] A JOURNEY BACK HOME

Make the vision happen & solve the problem (Design Doing)

Why?

How?

What?

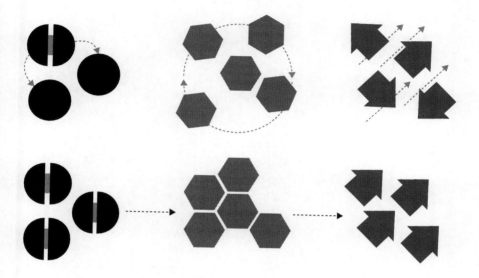

These people must share the same vision, using their business narrative to seek advantages and opportunities.

They are specialized in tearing things apart and must be shown how to put things together.

Understand how to make these people/elements work together, redefining what they do.

You need a way of thinking to explain why, how & what you do

It may seem like a philosophical approach, but being based on a "a way of thinking" is the only way to proceed in uncertain directions, especially when there are no validated processes or methods or best practices upon which to rely.

In a continuous transformative context like today, we can choose to move in two ways: the first is moving around short-cycle strategies, testing them, gathering feedback from the audience and defining the next step to take (commonly known as the **Lean Startup** approach); the second is to integrate this approach into a "way of thinking," a protocol that allows us to make choices without waiting for specific validation feedback to continue in the direction of optimal solutions.

Commonly in the market today we talk about Design Thinking or Strategic Thinking, but this does not mean that they are the only usable thoughts.

Each reality can create its own protocol by defining and answering three simple questions:

4. **Why?** (ex: Why do we do it? Why is it correct or incorrect?)

5. **How?** (ex: How do we do it? How does it work?)

6. **What? (ex: What do we do? What must happen?)**

Defining this protocol (way of thinking), sharing and using it are key factors for the occurrence of cohesion and rapidity in the evolution of every organic and participatory transformation.

More Insights
(Search the following sentence in Google to retrieve the link)

- **Simone Sinek - Start with why: how great leaders inspire everyone to take action**

Open minds with different narratives through ambassadors

We have already spoken extensively about business and operational narratives, but nevertheless they return in every context. This is because if we consider narratives as interfaces between two boundaries, each scenario of interlocutors has its own narrative.

Talking with a **CEO**, a **CMO**, or with a **Creative talent**, different narratives must be used to explain an idea, a strategy or an opportunity; narratives with which not only they are familiar, but that allow them to make an appropriate re-framing and contextualization of the impact that the idea can have on their daily life.

Systematic transformation requires a systematic method: scaling from 1 to 1000 is not an immediate, direct and linear process. **It is rather an exponential path.** Every individual or group of individuals is characterized by different backgrounds, perspectives, cultures, and for that reason, different narratives. A one-to-one relationship allows a refinement of the transformative narrative, ready to be scaled to another two-to-two ratio, and so on (and: 1x1, 2x2, 4x4, 8x8, 16x16, etc.). At each step, the transformative narrative not only becomes more efficient, but is refined and adapted to its audience creating confidence.

Open one mind, to open more minds: in this scenario at each step we create what we call ambassadors, for example people who enjoy different narratives from ours that allow us to influence and open minds that normally we would not succeed in reaching. Here in the transformative processes ambassadors belonging to different groups of the organization become decisive to activate a change: ambassadors in the C-suite, ambassadors in daily operations teams, ambassadors among talent, etc.

Help people put things together: open conversations

During operational transformations, the most frequent problem is the resilience of talent or, more generally, of all the groups belonging to the organization.

In every transformation, what happens is a reformulation of how to work differently, or simply, how things have to be put together differently. To do this, to understand it, to support it and to govern it, it is necessary to have an overview that's as complete as possible.

Very often, in a business context, teams & talent under the pressure of time, cost control and responsibility for results, we opt for old methods, validated, governable and reliable rather than taking new paths from an uncertain or unknown result thus slowing down the transformation.

To help the members of the organization overcome these barriers, open as many and constant multi-disciplinary conversation tables as possible, allow each member to understand other perspectives, frame the change more broadly and start to identify safe roads to follow.

More Insights
(Search the following sentence in Google to retrieve the link)

- **Barbara Kohm - The power of conversation**

- **HBR - Conversations can save companies**

- **HBR - Transforming the way we work**

Show a new way of doing: creating & share knowledge

It's important to have ambassadors with multi-level narratives and to open tables of conversation, but sometimes it is not enough to trigger an exponential transformation.

The last key factor is the sharing of knowledge. While I have already spoken in a previous chapter about the importance of setting up a **Knowledge Transfer System**, in this case, during the adoption phase of a new operating model, it becomes necessary to help the whole system to share all the knowledge that can be useful in unlocking deadlock situations and encouraging team resilience.

This knowledge often arises within the previously cited conversations that need to share their "discoveries" or insights with others.

In other cases, this knowledge can be found outside the organization itself, perhaps in extremely different contexts and businesses, but sharing the same factors and conditions. In many environments this knowledge is called a **business case**, in others **"lateral thinking."**

More Insights
(Search the following sentence in Google to retrieve the link)

- **Wikipedia - Lateral thinking**

- **HBR - How to capture knowledge without Killing it**

- **HBR - help employees create knowledge not just share it**

Be aware of what type of organization you are

According to **Frederic Laloux**, the author of *Reinventing Organizations: A Guide for Creating Organizations Inspired by the Next Stage of Human Consciousness*, "The days of the top-down hierarchy as the dominant organizational framework are numbered. Despite its continued preference by the current power elite, the bureaucratic management model is rapidly becoming both limited and obsolete now that the technology revolution has spawned a major inflection point in human history by unleashing the extraordinary and unstoppable phenomenon of distributed intelligence."

Using a color-coded typology inspired by the work of **Clare Graves**, and made popular by **Don Beck** and **Christopher Cowan** in their book *Spiral Dynamics*, Laloux outlines the evolution of four types of organizations over the last ten millennia and describes in detail the attributes and characteristics of a fifth and radically different emerging new organizational form. [1]

Each form of organization has different behaviors, systems and assumptions. The first four (Red, Amber, Orange and Green) are considered the historical types. From Red to Green, the quantity of bosses decreases progressively. [2]

The Teal organization is a revolutionary new management model that operates from the premise that organizations should be viewed as living organisms, and therefore, function more like complex adaptive systems than machines.

Accordingly, this organizational form is a structure of flexible and fluid peer relationships in which work is accomplished through self-managed teams.

In Teal organizations, there are no layers of middle management, very little staff, and very few rules or control mechanisms. Instead of reporting to single supervisors, people are accountable to the members of their teams for accomplishing self-organized collective goals.

As counterintuitive as it may seem, the elimination of controlling bosses typically enables a better controlled organization because, Laloux points out, "peer pressure regulates the system better than hierarchy ever could."

Thanks to the Internet, there's a new worldview, and it is revolutionizing the way we build organizations. Through dynamics, behaviors and complex system patterns we learn everyday by seeing platforms such as **Amazon**, **Google** or **Facebook** working and interacting with a distributed form of knowledge and consciousness, which are becoming more and more common in the management of any company.

Of course, each modern company/organization never fits completely into a specific color type, but we can identify each management system as a combination of colors. [3]

[1] EVOLUTION OF ORGANIZATIONS

[2] COLOR CODED TYPE OF ORGANIZATION STRUCTURES

0	MAGENTA	**None** (Wild)
1	RED	**Traditional Hierarchy** (Wolf pack)
2	AMBER	**Flatter organization** (Army)
3	ORANGE	**Flat organization** (Machine)
4	GREEN	**Flatarchies** (Family)
5	TEAL	**Holacratic organization** (Living organism)

[3] Samples modern organizations

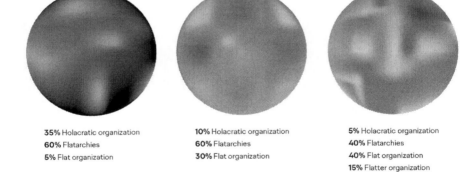

35% Holacratic organization
60% Flatarchies
5% Flat organization

10% Holacratic organization
60% Flatarchies
30% Flat organization

5% Holacratic organization
40% Flatarchies
40% Flat organization
15% Flatter organization

Let's start: seed, define & test

To trigger changes in these forms of sophisticated management organizations one must start with a change in the "way of thinking" for all the actors of the system.

A collective change of the "way of thinking" not only triggers an organic "change of doing," but empowers the managers in that area of the company with a more hierarchical organization to change their groups, stimulating conversation and knowledge exchange.

This ripple effect of external actions and the organic internal reactions, is the perfect way to approach this type of management structure with a hybrid form of organization.

The transformation process is based on a basic cycle of three factors:

7. **Seed** (open minds) – Introduce a new way of thinking, perspectives and everything else that's inspiring; triggering new questions and identifying new opportunities.

8. **Define** (how we work) – Reframe what we do, what the problems are that we are trying to solve and the solutions we can or should achieve.

9. **Test** (what we do) – Translate the new way of working, how to sell, how to change day-to-day activities, etc., at the business table.

Scale up: inject, adjust & consolidate

A systematic solution requires a systematic method. The scaling process will produce additional knowledge about the impact on the new organization's system on the company's business (re-frame). These discoveries will define the next scaling cycle strategy (new vision).

Seeding, Defining and Testing are part of the incremental transformation cycle to scale up the new system:

- **CYCLE 1** – **Inject**, to see different ways to work in different contexts

- **CYCLE 2** - **Adjust**, to observe

- **CYCLE 3** - **Consolidate**, to scale up

In the most sophisticated and autonomous area of the company the scaling cycle will impact with an increase in the frequency of changing behaviors, in the other areas more hierarchical, we will observe an increase in the size of quantity of changed behaviors.

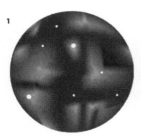

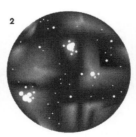

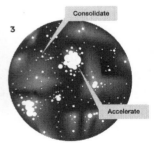

Brighter area grows faster in size | Darker area grows slower in size but faster in diffusion | Rapidly the change will be triggered...

Takeaways

Different narratives for the same vision are required.

–

Everyone must have a role.

–

Use design assumptions & methods to seek and adopt a solution.

–

A systematic solution requires a systematic method.

–

Transformation cannot be imposed. Transformation must be inclusive and participative.

References & notes

-

Thanks to my wife for supporting me
in this project.

Special thanks to

In alphabetical order: Alessandro Biggi, Alfonso Marián, Andrea Varalli, Antonio Iadarola, Dario Rigolin, Leandro Agrò, Ludovic Moulin, Marco de Veglia, Matteo Stanzani, Michele Budri, Paolo Bergamo, Sergio Mojoli.

Mentions

- Accenture - Pag 87, 91
- Airbnb - Pag 20, 63, 180, 190
- AKQA - Pag 97
- Alibaba - Pag 116
- Alistair Fuad-Luke - Pag 50
- Amazon - Pag 10, 20, 26, 62, 79, 91, 174, 190, 210
- Andrea Varalli - Pag 55
- Apple - Pag 10, 22, 79, 91, 116
- Arro - Pag 25
- Bill Moggridge - Pag 50
- Brian Lawson - Pag 50
- Buckminster Fuller- Pag 50
- Business Insider - Pag 86
- CapGemini - Pag 87
- CapitalOne - Pag, 91
- Car2Go - Pag 25
- Chapel Hill - Pag 174
- Charles Eames - Pag 118
- Christopher Cowan - Pag 209
- Clare Graves - Pag 209
- Cognizant - Pag 87
- CP+B - Pag 93
- Curb - Pag 25
- Dante Alighieri - Pag 76
- David Binder - Pag 116
- David Kelly - Pag 50
- Deborah Szabeko - Pag 50
- Deloitte - Pag 87, 91
- Dentsu - Pag 10
- Dollar Shave Club - Pag 21
- Don Beck - Pag 209
- Donald Schôn - Pag 50
- Droga5 - Pag 93
- Eero Saarinen - Pag 118
- Ezio Manzini - Pag 50
- Facebook - Pag 10, 79, 201
- Forbes - Pag 85
- Ford - Pag 21
- Frederic Laloux - Pag 195
- Glassdoor - Pag 31
- Google - Pag 10, 79, 210
- Harvard Business Review - Pag 84, 85
- Herbert A. Simon - Pag 50
- Honda - Pag 21

Mirco Pasqualini
January 2019
–

Email: mircopasqualini@me.com
–

Follow me
Twitter: @mircopasqualini
Linkedin: linkedin.com/in/mircopasqualini

Stay tuned, register at
mircopasqualini.com/books